ALL THE WAY

ALL THE WAY

The Life of Baseball Trailblazer
Maybelle Blair

KAT D. WILLIAMS

ROWMAN & LITTLEFIELD
Lanham • Boulder • New York • London

Rowman & Littlefield
Bloomsbury Publishing Inc, 1359 Broadway, 12th Floor, New York, NY 10018, USA
Bloomsbury Publishing Plc, 50 Bedford Square, London, WC1B 3DP, UK
Bloomsbury Publishing Ireland, 29 Earlsfort Terrace, Dublin 2, D02 AY28, Ireland
www.bloomsbury.com

First published in the United States of America 2025
Reprinted by Bloomsbury Academic 2025

British Library Cataloguing in Publication Information Available

Library of Congress Cataloging-in-Publication Data Available

ISBN 978-1-5381-8636-7 (cloth : alk. paper)
ISBN 978-1-5381-8637-4 (ebook)

For product safety related questions contact productsafety@bloomsbury.com.

∞™ The paper used in this publication meets the minimum requirements of
American National Standard for Information Sciences—Permanence of Paper for
Printed Library Materials, ANSI/NISO Z39.48-1992.

For my dad, TJ Williams—
thank you for teaching me to love the game and the characters who play it—
and
for Maybelle Blair, the greatest character of them all.

CONTENTS

INTRODUCTION

In August 2004, I eagerly yet nervously attended for the second time a reunion of the All-American Girls Professional Baseball League (AAGPBL) in Kalamazoo, Michigan. The previous year I had met some of the former players and was excited to meet more. I did. Many of them became my friends; all of them helped to change the course of my life—none more than Maybelle Blair. Our friendship was immediate and began as all things do where Blair is concerned, with a flourish and laughter.[1] As I went about finding my way around the throngs of people in the lobby of that year's reunion hotel, I noticed people playfully yelling up at a woman riding down the escalator. "Hey, there she is!" "Maybelle how'd they get you out of the casino?" I looked up to see a flashy, sunglasses-wearing woman with long painted fingernails and heard her contagious laugh. Maybelle Blair made her way through the lobby and within seconds began holding court among a group of girls and young women. I had no idea then how much this magnetic personality was going to affect my life.

And not only mine. In her later years, Blair became a public figure. To some she is a baseball star and a mentor to girls and women who seek opportunities in baseball. To the LGBTQ+ community, she is an inspiration. And she provides encouragement to an older generation who simply need to hear that you are never too old to make a difference. Maybelle's entire life was about baseball, women's baseball. About playing it, creating it, preserving it, and making it accessible to everyone. A *New York Times* headline read, "She inspired 'A League of Their Own.' At 95 she's far from done."[2] In a "Just Women's Sports" article, the reporter claimed, "Real-life inspiration for 'A League of Their Own' continues to push boundaries."[3] A *Sports Illustrated* reporter wrote, "From 'A League of Their Own' to building a museum of their own, Maybelle Blair inspires."[4] And, from "Entertainment Tonight," "a former player for the All-American Girls Professional Baseball League, Maybelle Blair broke down barriers for women, served as inspiration for the movie *A League of Their Own* and Prime Video's TV series by the same name." But she made her biggest splash when she came out "as a lesbian at 95 years old, after nearly eight decades of hiding."[5]

No one who knows her is surprised by these headlines, as Blair has been an inspiration to girls and women in all aspects of baseball for much of her life. But, as one of her young fans said of her newfound publicity, "it's about time the rest of the world learns what we have known for a long time, Maybelle Blair is awesome and none of us would be here without her, and others like her." Because she was an advisor on the new Amazon Prime series, *A League of Their Own*, and because she publicly "came out" at age ninety-five, her newfound popularity makes this the time to write her story. And this is her story.

Back at that AAGPBL reunion, the groups of fans were enthralled as Maybelle regaled them with stories of playing baseball. Seated nearby, I watched and listened until eventually another former player (who I learned later was Terry Donahue) rushed up to her. "Blair, what lies are you telling these girls?" she said. Laughing, Blair said, "Ah, my catcher, the little Canuck. Terry is from a place called Moose Jaw. You ever heard of such a thing?" They laughed, and, like a well-rehearsed comedy team, they both began telling the story about their meeting.

At the first reunion of the AAGPBL, in 1988, Blair and Terry met for what Terry thought was the first time. But, when a photographer called for the 1948 Peoria Redwings to line up for a picture, both stood up. Terry, always outspoken, cried, "Who are you?" "I was a pitcher in 1948," Blair answered. "You were my catcher." "I don't remember ever catching your curves," Terry said wryly. Clearly the story had been told many times, but their delight in sharing it with this new audience made it all the better. They both laughed at the memory, and, as I realized later, the inside joke.

Even though I had not been part of the group, as she turned to leave, Blair looked at me, smiled, and said, "You coming to the bar?" I did, and, from that time until now, I have been following Maybelle Blair to bars, baseball games, football games, casinos, tournaments, and premieres and along a winding path that led us to Rockford, Illinois, "the cradle of women's baseball."

As I prepared to write this book, Maybelle Blair and I sat down for an official interview. Within minutes I recognized a pattern in her life. When no baseball fields were at hand, she helped to build them. When there was no team, she created one. And when girls and women began demanding opportunities in the game they loved, she stepped up and spoke out, and she continues to do so. This dedication to baseball, both playing it and helping to create a space for others to be part of the game, reminded me of an Amelia Earhart quote that has meant a lot to me throughout my life:

> Some of us have great runways already built for us. If you have one, take off! But if you don't have one, realize it is your responsibility to grab a shovel and build one for yourself and for those who will follow after you.[6]

It struck her as it did me. "That is exactly what I've been doing, isn't it?" She asked. "Yes," I said. "It is." All she ever wanted was to play the game, but, in the 1930s, there were few opportunities for girls to play baseball, especially girls without the economic means to travel. Many softball teams were traveling teams, and, unless the team was fully sponsored, a girl might not be able to play. Still, Maybelle was determined. It was the first of her many efforts to get herself and other girls on a ball diamond. The number of girls and women who have benefited from Blair's efforts are way too numerous to count. From her early life growing up during the Great Depression through her baseball-playing days with the AAGPBL and, ultimately, as one of the country's best-known advocates for women's baseball, Maybelle Blair has spent most of her ninety-seven years digging runways and creating opportunities.

Blair's early connection to baseball and her quest to create it when it didn't exist were fostered by her family's love of the game and their determination to play it no matter what obstacles lay in front of them. She learned about the game from her father and brother but also learned from them never to just accept that there is no place to play or no team to join. Their approach was that, if one doesn't exist, build one. At a young age, Blair, along with her brother, Bud, helped to build a field across the street from their house, a field where both boys and girls played baseball. At the urging of her brother, by age six, she had learned how to keep a scorecard and did so for many Chicago Cubs games while listening to them on the radio. She readily agreed to chase fly balls when her brother and his friends took batting practice, and she even stood "stock still" in the batter's box as Bud honed his fastball. On that makeshift field alongside her father and brother, Maybelle continued to fine-tune her own baseball talent and, more importantly, her baseball intellect.

As the Great Depression suppressed the hopes and threatened the well-being of Americans, including those of the Blair family, baseball was never far from their daily lives. Even as her father struggled to find employment and her mother "worked miracles" to keep the family clothed and fed, the Blairs found ways to play, watch, and listen to baseball. The game made them happy, and, as Maybelle remembered, "it took our minds off of everything else. Even for a little while." Baseball and softball continued to be safe havens for Blair throughout her childhood. And, even later in life, when tragedy struck, it was baseball and the connections she made because of it that helped her through.

When she witnessed the unfair way girls who wanted to play softball were treated at her elementary school, Maybelle sought and received the help of a teacher. Together they convinced the school that girls should have a team too. They got one. As the boys enjoyed the excitement of traveling to another nearby school to play, Blair fumed because the girls could not. She changed that too. From elementary school through high school, Maybelle's push to play was relentless.

Graduating from high school did not dampen Blair's dedication to the game, but it did offer new possibilities on and off the diamond. Blair continued to play baseball and softball even after the United States entered World War II. Everyone stepped up to help, and that included women's softball teams. Playing with local teams, Maybelle traveled up and down the West Coast, playing at military bases. All this was done in an attempt to entertain the troops as they trained for war. Proud of the role she played in the war effort on the home front, Maybelle remembered that, during the war, she was also scared. She was proud that she and her teammates were doing their part and, as she said, "terrified that my brother would go to war." Thankfully, he didn't go to war, but Maybelle and her teams did keep playing softball at bases in California.

Because she played softball at a number of California military bases, her talent was visible. Because of that exposure Blair was recruited by a professional softball team, the Chicago Cardinals. Moving halfway across the country to play ball was an experience Maybelle never thought she would have, but she did, and it was life-changing. In the short time she played in Chicago, Blair made lifelong friends and while there caught the eye of coaches from the AAGPBL, a league created during World War II to entertain the baseball-loving, but weary, American citizenry. They asked her to try out and, despite a leg injury that slowed her, she was selected and became a Peoria Redwing in 1948. While her stint in the AAGPBL was brief, lasting only one year, the experience transformed her life in profound ways.

At the end of that 1948 season, injured and worried about her future, Maybelle did not return to the league. Rather she set out to develop a career that would support her. With the help of her brother, she was hired at Northrop Aircraft. But, even then, baseball and softball were a constant in her life. The thread that connects her entire life, baseball, was also woven through her thirty-five-year Northrop career. In addition to becoming the first female director of transportation, she also coached men's softball teams and formed the company's first softball team for women. It was after retirement from Northrop that she began her nearly full-time quest to create opportunities for girls and women in baseball. In the 1980s, she was reunited with the AAGPBL and became an active member of the Players Association. She, like other former players, also advised the makers of and even appeared in the 1992 Penny Marshall film *A League of Their Own*.

From working with the Players Association and realizing how important telling their stories was to others, she realized that women and girls in baseball needed more. They needed a home—a place to preserve their history, show it off, and use it to inspire generations to come. Out of that desire came the International Women's Baseball Center (IWBC). The creation of the IWBC and its transformation into a successful nonprofit represent another step in Maybelle's quest to support baseball for girls and women, to build the teams, the fields, and an international home where their history will be preserved and their dreams supported.

One lesson Maybelle's life teaches us is that there is always another goal to achieve, another way to make a difference in the world. Neither age nor detractors should stop us. In 2020, Maybelle began serving as a consultant for the new Amazon series *A League of Their Own*. The series focuses on, in addition to women's baseball, the social and cultural issues of the 1940s, such as gender and sexuality, issues that simply could not have been discussed in 1992, when the original movie came out. Blair's work with the series has brought her newfound fame and an even larger platform from which to spread her message: "Girls have always been part of baseball and we always will. People just don't seem to know that. Some of us are gay and some are not. Doesn't matter. Everyone has a place in the game."

Maybelle's life in and around baseball has inspired millions. Why it continues to do so is the focus of this book. Admittedly, Blair was never an all-star on the field, so this is not a typical baseball biography. It will not include her stats or feature reminiscences of her best game or of that one time she stole a base, hit a walk-off home run, or pitched a brilliant game.

Rather, this book, the baseball story of Maybelle Blair, is about way more than those numbers or even her performance on the field. Blair claimed that "no one loved the game more than me and no one learned more from it." For those reasons, and quite unconsciously at first, she spent much of her life carving a path for herself and others, a path that led directly to a baseball diamond. Later, "older and wiser" Maybelle did understand the importance of baseball beyond the fun and excitement of the game, and helping to create those opportunities for others became her life's work. How she went about doing that is the focus of this biography. As Maybelle said, "Baseball was never just a game, not for me and not for all those girls out there who begged to play. It is a lifeline for some of them, just like it is for boys. It is up to us to make sure they always have a place in baseball."

Whether you are a young girl searching for a place to play baseball or looking for a role model to help show you the way, for nearly a century Maybelle has been that person, the one building the fields, creating the teams, breaking barriers, and digging runways.

1

IT'S IN THE BLOOD

I had to love baseball. It was in the Blair blood.[1]

Being friends with Blair is not for the weak of heart. When you first meet her, it is as if the room shifts. She brings you into her world, and life is never the same. "That's how Texans are," she claimed when someone asked about her big, outgoing personality. "I'm from Texas. We do everything big and bold." "Yes," I reminded her later, "but you aren't from Texas." Blair was unfazed. "Well, my family was, so I'm a Texan too. Two of us Blairs died at the Alamo." There was no arguing that fact, and the California-born Maybelle Blair has continued to tell Texas-sized stories. Over the years and in every situation, those stories have been infused with energy, humor, and baseball.

★★★

Maybelle was correct that her family were Texans through and through. In 1834, the Scotland-born Samuel Blair registered for "a headright of land in James McGloin's colony of Texas."[2] Other Blair men followed. In 1835, Samuel's brother John Blair, great grandfather of Maybelle, registered as "a married man for a league of land in Texas."[3] But, when the brothers arrived, the community was in conflict. Texas was a province of Mexico at the time, but, in the same year that John arrived, it declared its independence from Mexico. The Blairs, and many other immigrants from the United States, became engaged in an all-out battle with Mexico over ownership of the land. In 1836, the Texans established the Republic of Texas, separate from both Mexico and the United States.

Angered that Mexico had lost control of the Texas province, Mexico's President Antonio López de Santa Anna vowed to retake the territory. With a large army, Santa Anna entered Texas in mid-February of 1836. By March of that year, the Texan army, made up of Anglo-American residents of Texas, was defeated at the Alamo. Both Samuel and John Blair were killed at the Alamo in March 1836. Their deaths became a source of pride for the Blair family and sealed their identity as Texans.

Skirmishes over control of Texas continued until the United States annexed Texas as its twenty-eighth state in 1845. This move led directly to the Mexican-American War, which the United States won in 1848. After the war, settlers were free to create communities in the new state of Texas. In 1854, a small community named Round Rock was formed near Austin. It lay on the banks of Bushy Creek and near a large round rock that marked a low-water crossing for wagons and horses. The crossing and the town were part of the famed Chisolm Trail. It was near Round Rock that the remaining Blair family acquired and farmed large parcels of land. Eventually the family expanded and moved to Hamilton, Texas, which was just eighty miles from Round Rock. Maybelle's parents, George Blair and Iva Patterson, met in Hamilton, and that was where Maybelle's baseball roots were planted.

Baseball showed up in Texas around the time of the Civil War and spread rapidly as communities such as Round Rock and Hamilton embraced the game. On small fields carved out of farmland and planned fields with lines and dugouts, Texans such as the Blairs played the game. "My whole family played," said Maybelle. "My father and his brothers and cousins all fell in love with baseball." So much so that they created a baseball team known as the Blair Nine. The Blair Nine played other local teams around the area, and on game days much of the community showed up to watch. Often women would "bring fried chicken and prepared jars of lemonade for the game and people came from miles around to see the local nine take on another town team."[4]

The Blair family was not alone in their love for the game. This scene played out all over Texas as baseball's popularity spread among Texans of every class, but especially among the state's farmers. The game provided diversion from a hard life, and it was inexpensive to play. A number of the first baseball games in Texas were played in pastures where sheep and cattle helped keep the grass short enough to play.[5] It was in that context that the Blairs learned to love and to play baseball. When they moved to California during the Great Depression, they brought that baseball passion with them.

Before Maybelle was born, the entire Blair family moved from Texas to Redondo Beach, California. As soon as the Blairs arrived, Maybelle's father and two of his brothers joined a local baseball team. She does not remember the name of the team, but Maybelle remembered that during one of their games her cousin, a boy she never knew, climbed an electric tower. With barely hidden contempt, Blair recalled, "He climbed up there and got himself electrocuted. They had to stop the game. Stupid kid." Maybelle was told that story as a cautionary tale, but for her the message was about what you should be doing during a baseball game: watching it or playing in it—not off climbing some pole. By then, she was fully engaged in the game of baseball.

Maybelle was born in Redondo Beach on January 16, 1927, and that is where she fell in love with baseball. As Maybelle says, "I was born with baseball in my blood. My mother's breasts had baseballs instead of milk!" Both her brother, George Jr. (Bud), born in Texas, and Maybelle grew up with the game and learned to love it, watch it, and play it. Some of her first memories are of watching her father and his brothers play baseball. When the hardship of the Great Depression seemed overwhelming to the Blairs, they, as their relatives before them had, turned to baseball. In describing her childhood during the Depression, Maybelle was clear about the struggles of the time. But with every story about hardship, Blair had a baseball memory to match. Even though she was much smaller, and a girl, Maybelle's father and brother included her whenever they could. Eager to please them and to be part of the game, Maybelle jumped at every chance. "Baseball was what we all did, what we all wanted to do. It's what saved us," Maybelle said. "We all loved it, and it didn't cost much to play in those days. So, we did."

Like many families, the Blairs worked hard during those economically difficult times and made do with what they had. Maybelle's father worked breaking up rock in a quarry for a dollar a day, and "he was lucky to get that," Blair said. "Food was scarce. My mother raised a garden, and we had a cow, and then we raised chickens, rabbits, and pigeons so we could eat. And we had fruit trees. I remember once my mother and our next-door neighbor split a loaf of bread so they could make sandwiches for our fathers' lunch. It was terrible." Maybelle also helped secure food when she could. "We were next to a bean field, and they'd thrash beans, and I would take my sack when I was a little girl and go pick up the beans left behind and bring them home. My mother would make bean soup. That's how we survived."

Maybelle's mother, a creative seamstress, made clothes for her family and others. "She'd make a whole dress and maybe a pair of pants for a dollar each." Blair said. Iva Blair kept her family clothed by using feed sack material to make their clothes. Maybelle understood even from an early age how hard her parents worked to support the family and appreciated the homemade clothes she and her brother wore, saying, "I loved my feed sack dress because mother made it, and I loved my little underpants that matched." Her appreciation for the clothes did not mean she always took care of them, though.

In addition to everyday clothes, Iva also made Maybelle clothes for special occasions. "One Easter, she made me the most beautiful little Easter dress. And I thought I was the prettiest thing in that little new dress. We were going to go to church later so my mother told me to be sure to stay home. But no. I wanted to show off my little Easter dress. I was so proud and thought it was so cute. So, I went across the street to the neighbor's house. And they had these little baby ducklings. Well, you know what happened. I picked it up and that duck let loose. Duck poop went all the way down my dress and my little new socks into my shoes." Maybelle ruined her newly made dress, but even worse was the regret she still feels, ninety years later, that she destroyed the dress her mother made. "I never listened," she said. "But then sometimes that's a good thing, you know, never taking no!" First her family and then girls and women who love baseball all benefited from Blair's refusal to accept no.

Throughout the 1930s the Blair family struggled economically, but, as Maybelle said, "us kids always had what we needed. We had food and clothes, lots of love, and baseball." Blair's parents loved baseball as much as Maybelle and Bud did. Perhaps because of that love and understanding of the game they were able to use baseball to teach their kids important life lessons: honesty, integrity, the importance of physical activity, and, in Maybelle's case, to always follow your dreams. As their ancestors did before them, the Blairs either found or created fields and teams on which to play. "If one didn't exist, we'd build one," Maybelle said. Blair's father and brother solicited Maybelle's help in creating a "real baseball field" out of an empty lot across from their house. She eagerly accepted.

The family worked on the field when they could, at weekends and after school and work, and soon it was done. "They went out and got rid of all the weeds and plowed it. It was all dirt, but it was wonderful." Once the field was finished the whole neighborhood benefited from having it.

Blair recalled one of the first games played on the field. "During one of the first games between our neighborhood team and the town next to us, one of the foul balls came over the fence and hit me in the nose and broke it. See, right there?" Maybelle's nose was broken that day, but her baseball memories and dreams were not.

One of Maybelle's roles in creating the field was to sit on an old gate that Bud was using to drag the field. "Bud would say, 'sis, come on out here and sit on this gate so I can drag the field.' I did anything he asked so I did it. Just a little thing. I'd get on the gate; he'd get on the tractor and off we'd go. I was flying around back there, covered in dust, him hollering, 'Sit still. Hang on.'" Recalling that memory through laughter, Blair said, "It is a wonder he didn't kill me. All the stuff he got me into. But I loved every cockeyed minute of it." Some days Maybelle actually got to play on the field. On what she called the "best days," Bud invited Maybelle to chase fly balls when his team took batting practice, or, if he was practicing his fast ball, he'd have her stand in the batter's box and pretend to be a hitter. "My father would be his catcher, and he'd haul off and throw that ball as hard as he could. There I was, little Maybelle standing in, praying he wouldn't hit me." She said with a laugh, "I was on a baseball field, though, so I didn't care that much what I was doing there."

The whole family thought Bud was going to be a major-league ball-player, and, according to Blair, they all helped when he needed to practice. "Somehow, they even saved enough money to buy him a baseball uniform. I don't know how they did it, but like I said, we did without food before baseball. So, they bought this uniform. He would strut around acting like a big leaguer. He warned me, though, to never touch his uniform." Maybelle coveted that uniform, and she wanted to be a big leaguer too, although 1930s American society would not have supported girls wearing a baseball uniform or playing with boys on an organized team. Blair begged and begged her mother to let her try on the uniform when Bud wasn't home. Understanding Maybelle's own baseball dreams and love for the game, Iva Blair fueled her daughter's baseball dreams when she stood watch while Maybelle wore the uniform around the house. "When he would go off to play or go to someplace with the boys to play baseball where he didn't wear his uniform, I would go in and put on that uniform. I thought I was a big-time ball player. My mother would keep looking out the window to make sure he wasn't coming. Because he would've died if he knew I was wearing his uniform." Aside from sneaking around the house in his uniform, Maybelle would not have done anything to hamper Bud's path to baseball. "I thought he was the best thing on two legs."

Maybelle's role in supporting Bud's baseball dreams continued off the field too. When she was about eight, Bud taught Maybelle how to use an official scorecard. Then he parked her by the radio so she could keep score for the Chicago Cubs' games. Between innings, Maybelle went to the ball field where Bud was playing with his friends to update them on the game. "I was so proud he wanted me to help him, and I got to be part of baseball. Since I was born, that's all I ever wanted: to play baseball. Both Bud and my father usually included me in some way. I didn't care what they asked me to do as long as I was on that field." From her earliest memories, baseball was a constant source of fun, and during the Depression it was a haven where the difficulties of the Blairs' lives did not intrude.

Starting school—not being home with her mother and not being just across the street from that field—was difficult for Maybelle, but then she discovered recess. "I found out that kids got to play games at recess, so I was okay with going." Soon, however, Maybelle realized that those games did not include baseball for the girls. "I did not like it that girls weren't invited to play baseball like the boys. I had always been included when my family played, and I just didn't understand. I knew Bud's school team even played games against other schools so I said, why can't we?" Taking matters into her own hands, Maybelle rounded up girls from the school she knew could play softball and created a softball team. In the 1930s and 1940s, girls were told to play softball as baseball had become a game for boys and men. The common notion was that softball was a girl's version of baseball and was made just for them. Softball, however, was not invented as a girl's sport. In fact, it was created in 1887 in Chicago, by men who wanted a game that could be played indoors during the winter. Softball was played all over the country, but, until the 1930s, there was little mention of women playing any sport. At the time, men thought sports were too strenuous for women. After women won the right to vote in 1920 and as the nation began to recover from the Great Depression in the 1930s, softball's popularity began to grow among girls and women. In 1939, an estimated sixty million fans watched softball games, which is ten million more than watched baseball. While both men and women played softball, women's games were more popular.[6]

Girls like Blair accepted their fate and turned their attention to the increasingly popular game of softball. "I loved baseball and played when I could but for us to have a team of our own, it had to be softball. So, that's what we did." Proud of her team and her role as coach, Blair said,

"I practiced those girls. There I was, a little thing, eleven, I think. Boy, I practiced those girls, though. I lined them up and played pepper or practiced in some way. And then I went to the teacher and pleaded for them to let us play other schools." Fortunately for Maybelle, her fifth-grade teacher Mrs. Glidden liked her. "I had a crush on her, and she liked me because I was a big loudmouth, I guess, and she liked sports too." Mrs. Glidden was Maybelle's first crush—but "not the last," she added. "I just loved her, and I would sit next to her when I could. I was her pet, I think, and I loved every minute of it." Whether it was because of her own interest in sports or Blair's determination, Mrs. Glidden supported her efforts and agreed to contact the nearby Perry School about "having a little contest between the girls." They said yes. She piled part of the team into her car, and somebody else took the rest. "There were two carloads of us. Off we went over to Perry, and then Perry came back over to our school and played us later on." The games took place after school on what Blair called "rough little softball diamonds," and, despite the state of the field or how much experience her team had, for two years Blair coached and played on her school's softball team.

Mrs. Glidden was also Maybelle's sixth-grade teacher and continued to support her dreams of playing ball. She introduced Maybelle to the niece of Bob Meusel. Meusel played in the major leagues for eleven seasons, from 1920 through 1930. He was best known as a member of the Yankees championship team nicknamed the "Murderers' Row." Bob Meusel's niece, whose name Maybelle did not remember when she was interviewed, became Maybelle's friend. It was exciting to have as a friend another girl who knew as much about and loved baseball as much as she did. "That girl kept talking about Bob and how good he was and how she was one of the few girls who could play. We became friends. It was nice for me to know some girls that really liked baseball. I was happy that Mrs. Glidden got us together." Other than Meusel's niece, Maybelle only remembers the girls she deemed "good enough to really play. Lily Matthews was very good and Rosemary McQue. They're the only ones I remember that was any good." Despite a lack of raw talent in both the fifth and sixth grades, Maybelle did what generations of Blairs had done—she created a team and a place for her and the other eleven- and twelve-year-old girls at South School to play.

Starting with her father and mother and continuing with Mrs. Glidden, Maybelle was fortunate to have adults who indulged her love of baseball. No doubt all of them understood that it was unusual for girls in the 1930s to be that enthusiastic about the game. But, for varied reasons, both her parents and her teacher supported and facilitated that passion.

Because of the Blair family connection to baseball, it made sense to her parents that Maybelle would also have a connection to the game. It is true that they expected Bud, not Maybelle, to become a professional athlete, but, when the opportunity presented itself to Maybelle, they supported her. Her teacher Mrs. Glidden was "a fan of sports" and, as Maybelle said, "I think she liked me. I did things she couldn't do." Did she envy Maybelle's chance to play baseball, the naivete it took to demand the school let the girls play, or was she simply a supportive teacher? Blair was unsure, but, whatever the reasons, she was grateful to her teacher and to her parents. Few girls in the 1930s would have had the level of support it took to persevere in their quest to play baseball.

From playing to watching local games or their beloved Angels, the Blairs' life was consumed by baseball. "When we could save enough pennies, we'd go to see the Angels. We always went on Sunday because it was a doubleheader. Me and my brother used to have a contest to see who would spot the lights at Angel Stadium first. Avalon and 42nd street. I'll never forget it. I couldn't wait to get to the ballpark. We'd walk by the concession stand and you could smell those hot dogs. We couldn't afford them. But I loved that smell. Still do." Maybelle loved everything about the ballpark, the smells, the sound of a bat hitting the ball, and the excitement of watching the players—any players. "If we couldn't go see the Angels on a Sunday, we'd pile in that old car and drive over to Redondo or someplace. You'd see a field of people, boys usually playing baseball. We'd stop and hop out to watch." Sometimes the players themselves were memorable. "I got to see Babe Ruth at Angel Stadium," Blair said. "I was little, maybe seven or eight, when his Babe Ruth all-star traveling team came, and we went. I'll never forget it." Whether it was watching famous players or the boys they found on a Sunday drive, Maybelle loved those Sundays. Her family bonded on those afternoons, watching baseball, and Maybelle's love for the game became forever entwined with her love for family.

As the country struggled through the Great Depression and rolled toward war, Maybelle remembered, "We didn't notice much of a difference in our lives from 1939 to 1941. It was all baseball and softball, working to make ends meet, and more baseball." But on December 7, 1941, their lives and the lives of all Americans changed. "Oh gosh," Blair said. "I remember Pearl Harbor. We were sitting at the dining room table when the news came out." The Blair family had experienced the loss of loved ones in World War I, and Maybelle's parents had lost three children at an early age, so they were immediately afraid about the possibility of

Bud going to war. "Well, first of all, we didn't have to worry, I guess. He was working for Northrop Aircraft, and, because of the job working in an airplane factory, they wouldn't let him go. Every time it would come up, Northrop would give him excuses." While working at Northrop, Bud did what Blairs had done before him—he joined the company baseball team and managed both to work for the war effort and to play baseball.

Bud's family members were thankful that Bud's work at Northrup gave him an excuse not to join the military, but, like most young men, Bud wanted to join. He had what Blair called "infantile paralysis" when he was young.[7] Although he did not suffer the level of paralysis often associated with the disease, he did suffer from stomach issues throughout his entire life. Maybelle remembered that "certain odors made him sick." He could have gotten an exemption but chose not to seek one. Because the war continued longer than expected and because jobs necessitated by the war were increasingly filled by women, men who were otherwise exempt were accepted at military recruiting stations. Bud was one such recruit. He was anxious to go, so he did not reveal his condition. Maybelle recalled, "Off he went to training, they did these big maneuvers, and he got sick." Bud was taken to the hospital, where the doctors discovered his medical history. It was not just Bud's health but also his mother's actions that kept him from going to war. Concerned about her only surviving son, Iva Blair wrote a letter to President Roosevelt. She told the president about what had happened to her other children and that Bud had suffered from infantile paralysis as a child. She asked Mr. Roosevelt to please keep her son away from the war. Maybelle remembered that "Mr. Roosevelt wrote a letter to my mother saying, 'Mrs. Blair, don't worry. He'll never have to go overseas. I promise you.'" And he didn't. According to Maybelle, Bud never knew his mother had written the president on his behalf. "She told me, 'Don't ever let him know that I sent that letter.'" It's not clear if Bud found out.

In the end, Bud entered the army and served stateside. While he was saved from going to war, serving stateside also had a life-altering impact on Bud. He was offered a discharge from the army, but he did not want it. The army agreed to keep him in service but put him in charge of recreation. His training started in Texas, but he was soon stationed at Fort Riley, Kansas. In what must have seemed like the best luck, while at Fort Riley, Bud played on its baseball team. In what Maybelle remembers as a freak accident, Bud's dream of playing professional baseball ended at Fort Riley. Bud was up to bat when the sun blinded him temporarily and, in an effort to shield his eyes, he put his arm up. The pitched ball shattered his arm, ending any hope he had of playing professionally. Bud stayed in the army until the war's end. Continuing to supervise recreation, he also tried to play baseball or softball at any level he could. But his career aspirations were over.

During the war, life and her focus on baseball and softball did not change much for Maybelle. "I just kept pushing to play and, when I got up to the other school, higher grades [high school], I got a team up there, too. They didn't have any softball teams for girls, so I formed teams." Although Mrs. Glidden was not there to help, Maybelle managed to convince her new school, Lawndale, to let girls play. During the two years she was there, they had what she remembered to be "some nice little teams." While she was happy to have the school team, Maybelle was flattered when the coach of a team called "Mr. West's Sweet Shop" sought her out. Mr. West was not only a huge fan of girls' softball but also the sponsor of the team. He was an even bigger fan of Blair's, so in addition to putting her on his team he also hired her at his candy shop. That was Maybelle's first job. "Mr. West hired me to be a soda jerk." She said with a laugh, "He probably regretted it later." The shop was directly across the street from the town's only theater, so a lot of the teenagers in town congregated at the sweet shop. "I became very popular with the high-school kids because I was always giving away free sodas." Blair worked at the sweet shop every weekend for a year, unless there was a softball game. Mr. West always let her off work to play a game. "It was his team, and he would rather have me playing than giving away sodas!" While playing for Mr. West, Maybelle was also recruited to play for what she remembered to be "semipro softball teams at first, then professional teams." Her career of semiprofessional and then professional softball had begun.

2

RECRUITED

During the first couple of years of World War II, softball, especially women's softball, was growing in popularity and in usefulness on the home front. Looking back on those years, Maybelle remembered that, when she first started playing semiprofessional softball, there was a larger number of girls' traveling softball teams than before. Her memory is correct. Softball was growing exponentially throughout the late 1930s and into the 1940s, especially in areas like California where the weather was often mild, which provided a lot of opportunities to play. In the 1940s, Southern California produced a number of very talented women's fast-pitch softball teams. The teams competed at a high level, and some even barnstormed across the country.[1] In 1944, Hollywood actress Gladys Lloyd recruited a group of women war workers to form a softball team to entertain servicemen stationed at California's desert training bases. Soon thereafter this group became the Pasadena Ramblers.

"I got recruited to play for the Pasadena Ramblers," Maybelle said. "This team was a bunch of girls traveling all over to the bases and playing softball teams on the bases. Most were men's teams and we beat them sometimes too." The Ramblers and other women's softball teams traveled up and down the California coast, playing games. "We went to all the forts and all the bases, from San Pedro to all the forts. One of the places where we played had the German prisoners out in a compound. They got to watch us play. They were just hollering and carrying on." As always, Maybelle was happy playing and loved traveling around to the military bases, but playing in front of the German prisoners of war made her a little nervous. "We kept saying, 'well, it's okay. They are behind the fence. We should be safe.'" Laughing about that memory eighty years later, Blair said, "They were just young kids. We didn't realize it then, but they were more afraid than we were." Even fear was not going to keep Maybelle and her team from playing a game, ever.

For the first two years of war, Maybelle continued to play for the Pasadena Ramblers and enjoyed her high-school years. There was a war going on, and, like her parents, Maybelle also worried about Bud, but, as she remembered, "I had a ball in high school. Most people say they hated it, but not me. Lots of reasons," she said with a chuckle. Maybelle had her first and only boyfriend in high school. "He was the best ballplayer, and I was the best athlete in school for girls. That was it really. Then I met this girl, my senior year, named Helen Actheberg. Somehow, I had a little crush on her and vice versa. I don't know how it happened. To this day I don't know how it happened. I can't remember, but we had a little to do as my first episode." Characterizing her first sexual experience with a girl as an "episode" may seem odd to twenty-first–century readers, but for seventeen-year-old Maybelle that experience was frightening. In what is an all-too-familiar refrain, Blair said "Oh, God. I thought that we were the only two people like that in the world." For most of Maybelle's seventeen years, baseball and softball had been the center of her life. But she had no idea that it would also open another entire world to her.

She may not have been ready to accept her place in that world, but the combination of that crush, playing softball with the Ramblers, and working a summer job at Northrop Aircraft as a "go get me" girl—a job we might call a gopher today—gave Maybelle a much wider view of the world than she would have had under the watchful eye of her mother in Lawndale. Despite feeling like she and Helen were the only girls who "were like that" (attracted to their own sex), the experience with Helen made Blair more aware so, once she began playing softball with the Ramblers and was introduced to a larger community of other lesbians, she began to explore that part of herself. Blair's job at Northrop was mostly running errands and delivering messages within the company, though she also worked "in public relations making scrapbooks with all the pictures of the aircraft coming in." That summer employment set the stage for what would be a career at Northrop. But, most importantly at the time, it helped her family financially.

Before the war started, Blair's father George had been hired by the county to supervise the building of a park by the Works Progress Administration (WPA). That meant that by the mid-1940s the family had a little more money and George had stable employment. The job also allowed them to foster their connection to baseball. George Blair was hired by a man named Mr. Weber. Maybelle was not sure exactly who Mr.

Weber was but described him as "some big wheel in the county of Los Angeles. He liked my father because he knew he was a good worker. So, they hired him to be in charge of building the Ladera Park in Inglewood, California." George supervised the WPA workers hired by the county to create what is now called Ladera Park.

Working at a park all day and with men who were, like George, interested in baseball or simply desperate for a fun outlet gave George another way to create baseball opportunities for himself and his workers. After working at the park for some time, he gathered enough of the workers to form a team. "Those workers were doctors and lawyers and everything in between, and he had them all out there playing baseball," Blair remembered. The team practiced or played games on the weekends when its members were not working. George played catcher for the team, and Maybelle remembers the fun of watching him play. "They played all over the Los Angeles area, Redondo, Hermosa Beach, all over. Sometimes they played other park teams and sometimes semipro teams." By the time World War II ended, meanwhile, Maybelle's brother Bud was back playing baseball for Northrop Aircraft, where he worked full-time. In those years, it didn't matter where they played. Iva, Bud, and Maybelle packed up lunch and headed to the ballpark.

In 1947, Maybelle embarked on experiences she never knew were possible. While playing with the Ramblers, Maybelle got noticed by other traveling softball teams. In 1947, the Chicago Cardinals, a team that played in the National Girls Baseball League (NGBL) (which was actually a softball league), recruited Blair to play in the Chicago-based league. The NGBL was founded in 1944 by Forest Park, Illinois, contractor Emery Parichy; Charles Bidwill, who was the owner of the Chicago Cardinals football team; and politician Ed Kolski. Parichy had built Parichy Stadium in Forest Park in 1934 and owned a softball league, the Metropolitan League. Parichy and Bidwell hired Red Grange to run the league.[2]

The NGBL consisted of teams from the greater Chicago area and regularly drew over five hundred thousand fans annually. Unlike the AAGPBL, the NGBL kept the traditional underhand softball-pitching format throughout its existence. The NGBL evolved out of the high-quality amateur Chicago Metropolitan Softball League and attracted some of the best women athletes in the country during the 1930s and 1940s.[3] "I was playing softball in Inglewood, and the scout came out just like in the movie [*A League of Their Own*] showed. He told me he would like for me to go play softball for the Chicago Cardinals. I told him no because of my mother. I didn't want to leave my mother. I was a mother's girl. So, I was afraid." Maybelle had never spent a night away from her mother, not even at a friend's house, so the thought of traveling halfway across the country terrified her. "I was so spoiled," Maybelle said, "I couldn't even comb my hair. My mother did everything for me. I didn't have to do anything. She told me once that she had to work so hard all her life. She wanted me to enjoy mine." She did.

The scout talked to Iva and George and assured them that the Chicago Cardinals were a professional softball team and that Maybelle would be looked after while she was in Chicago. Always protective of the team's image, the scout wanted to reassure the Blairs that none of those "manly lesbians" who played for some softball teams would threaten their daughter. "We'll protect her from those girls," he told Iva. "My mother didn't know what the hell he was talking about, and I didn't either." It wouldn't take long for her to find out. But meanwhile, Maybelle was simultaneously scared by and excited at the possibility of playing professional softball and being so far away from home. But, with her "old mitt and a small bag with clothes" Maybelle got on a train headed east. Once she was in Chicago, representatives of the team picked her up and dropped her off at a hotel. "I was in this room, and I'd never been away from my mother. Scared to death. I pushed the dresser up against the door of the hotel room and had me about three balls. If anybody dared come in that door, I'd whack them. I could throw pretty hard." After a few sleepless nights, she had to tell her coach that she was too scared.

In order to make Maybelle feel more secure, the team gave her a roommate, Mary Lou Swanagon. Swannie, as the other ballplayers called her, had come from the AAGPBL to join the Cardinals. The league had started in 1943, and, while it was going strong in 1947, many of the women who were softball players before joining the league decided to return to softball. The pay was better, and they were afraid the longer distances between the bases in baseball would cause them to injure their arms.

Swannie became Blair's roommate, and, more importantly, she introduced her to the gay world. "She and I became very good friends and did a lot together. We were friends until the day she died." Swannie and Blair were so close that two of the other players who were gay assumed they were a couple and sought them out. The couple invited Swannie and Maybelle to their room, just for a visit. "Mary Lou was a little smarter than I was on account of the All Americans. A lot of those girls were gay, so she had experiences. She knew about it, and I didn't. We went over there, and this girl latched on to Mary Lou and this other girl sort of liked me. We went home!" Maybelle was young and inexperienced and, even though she had "episodes" prior to arriving in Chicago, the openness of those older women frightened her. That experience increased Blair's uncertainty about being on her own, but it did open her eyes to a whole new world.

Somehow, George Wragg, or Sarge as the team called him, got wind of the incident involving the other two women, and, because of the team's promise to Blair's mother that the team would protect her, he said to Blair, "I got to move you two." "So, he sent us to the Hyde Park Hotel in Chicago, out on the east side, away from everybody," Blair explained. True to his word, he called a team meeting in which he told team members, "I promised Mrs. Blair that, if anything happened, I would send Maybelle home." Marge Smith, who was the team's center fielder and a schoolteacher in Chicago, offered to be responsible for Blair and Swannie. "Don't worry about it, Sarge," she said. "I'll see that they are all okay. I'll be in charge." Sarge did not send Maybelle home but did arrange for Marge to keep a close eye on her.

One night when they did not have a game, Marge invited Blair and Swannie to her house for a sleepover. When they arrived, Marge showed Swannie to her room and told Maybelle that she would sleep with her. Once in bed Marge put her arm around Blair and kissed her on the cheek. "I pretended to be asleep," Maybelle said. "I didn't fall for all that crap because she didn't appeal to me at all in any direction." Blair was not attracted to Marge, but she did know that Sarge would listen to her and that, if she wanted to stay in Chicago, she could not insult Marge. A few weeks later, Marge wanted to spend the night in Swannie and Maybelle's room. They had twin beds, and Marge insisted on sleeping with Blair. "She did the same thing again and the next day I said, 'Look Swannie I cannot handle this any longer. You have got to help me out. Next time she comes over, she's got to sleep with you.' Thank God she did and then she turned her attention to Swannie." Maybelle's introduction to Chicago's gay scene was only just beginning.

One weekend night, after a game, Swannie and Maybelle were deciding what to do when they overheard some of the girls saying they were going to a tavern called Tolan's. They had no idea what Tolan's was, but they did not want to sit at the hotel, so they decided to go. With no idea what they were getting into, they got directions to the bar, and figured out how to ride the El (the elevated train) to Tolan's. "We leaped on the streetcar, and the conductor says, 'Well, where are you girls going?' I proudly said, 'Oh, we're going to Tolan's.' He says, 'You're going where?' 'We're going to Tolan's.' He knew what it was." Pretty soon they found out too.

Maybelle and Swannie arrived at Tolan's completely unsure what to expect, but neither expected the greeting they got. "When we walked in there, they all screamed out, 'Oh no, go home. This is a gay bar.'" For a few minutes Maybelle, in complete shock, stood staring. "I just kept thinking, oh my God. There's a gay bar. Oh my God, they're all gay. I thought I was the only one in the world." She described that moment as being like time slowed and all those women swirled around her as though in a dream. It was both the most exciting and most terrifying moment of her life.

In the mid-1940s, being gay, visiting gay bars, or even acknowledging one's sexuality could be dangerous. During the war, homosexuals had increasing opportunities to find each other and form communities, local bars, and social organizations away from the restrictions of small towns or family pressure. Many people stayed in the port cities when they returned from war or eventually moved to urban areas where it was easier to live their lives without fear.[4] But, by the late 1940s, when Maybelle was in Chicago, an open and often violent purge of homosexuals, known as the Lavender Scare, had begun. The country was in the midst of a more general sex-crime panic, stirred by a few highly publicized cases, and one result was a "Sex Perversion Elimination Program" that targeted gay men for arrest and intimidation. In 1948, Congress acknowledged a need for laws that treated "sexual psychopaths." Their solution resulted in a law that allowed for the arrest and punishment of people who acted on same-sex desire.[5] The codification of homophobia led to homosexuality being widely perceived as a subversive threat to the country. It was in this context that Maybelle Blair walked into Tolan's bar.

As people who fought in the war did, Maybelle used a newfound freedom to explore her own sexuality. "There was no turning back," she said. "Once I knew I wasn't the only one and that so many other girls were like me, I started to live." Maybelle met a number of the players from the AAGPBL while in Chicago. "Some of those girls knew some of our girls, so a lot of us became friends. That's how I first met Tiby and Snookie," she remembered. When the 1947 season ended, Maybelle headed home to California. After a month Swannie came to visit Blair in California. The pair didn't have much to do most days, so they went to Brookside Park, where some of the California girls who played in the AAGPBL worked out with one of their coaches, Bill Allington.

At Brookside Park, Maybelle met more of the AAGPBL players. At times she and Swannie joined in and played and worked out with them. It was both a fun and a productive way to spend the offseason and another first for Maybelle. Snookie and Tiby, who were a bit older and certainly more experienced, took Swannie and Maybelle to a gay bar called the IF Club. "It was in Los Angeles, the first gay bar out here that I ever been to. I was scared to death. Absolutely scared out of my cotton-picking shoes to do this."

Even though she and Swannie spent time at Tolan's in Chicago, Los Angeles was closer to home, and the possibility of being "found out" by family and friends was greater. Still, she remembers fondly her first visit to a gay bar in Los Angelos. The IF Club was a well-known bar that opened in 1942 and that played a big role in the queer landscape of mid-century Los Angeles. Known as one of the earliest lesbian bars in the country, it was located at 8th and Vermont, welcomed white, Black, and Latina women, and catered to a working-class clientele. Initially, Maybelle was scared to go but was also intrigued, so, when Snookie said, "Oh don't worry, you'll know a lot of the girls," Maybelle agreed. Despite the fact that she felt more worldly and thought that she was more prepared for her first trip to the IF Club, the women at the bar were shocked when she walked in. "I was younger than the rest of them and I was good at keeping those things secret. I had not been to a bar around home so most of the girls didn't know. Practically the whole bar turned around and said, 'What are you doing here? Get out of here, do you know what kind of bar this is?'" She did know, of course, and fondly remembers the shocked looks of those women when she walked in with Snookie and Tiby. Her teammates knew the dangers of being there and, because of her youth, wanted to protect Blair. She was having none of it. With what she remembered as "a mix of fear on the inside and excitement on the outside," she walked into that bar as if she owned it. "They said, 'Why are you here? What are you doing?' 'Well, I'm visiting,'" Blair said as she strolled past them.

From her first trip to Chicago for the 1947 season to the end of the offseason, Maybelle continued to practice, play softball whenever possible, work part time at Northrop, and visit the IF Club. She and Swannie were glad to have each other as both cautiously explored a new world. But, as she and Swannie explored the Los Angeles gay scene, Maybelle was always conscious of her family and how important it was to protect them. She maintained the same relationship with them she had before going to Chicago: watching or playing baseball together whenever possible and always helping with the family finances. By this time, George had already worked for Los Angeles County for several years. When the construction of the park was completed, George moved from supervising the WPA workers to the position of park supervisor. Since there was no longer a need for WPA workers who represented a wide range of education levels, the county took the opportunity to upgrade employment requirements. To work in a managerial or supervisory role, employees had to either have a high-school degree or be able to pass an equivalency test. With only a sixth-grade education, George was unable to pass the test and was fired. Maybelle remembers that they called it "retired" rather than fired, but the reality was that he did not retire; nor did he want to leave the job. A much younger man, one that George had hired and trained, took over his position. The loss of his job was hard on Maybelle's father, physically and mentally. "It nearly killed him," she said. He loved his job, the physical work and the connections to baseball teams and fields. Sadly, George's opportunities to play baseball on an organized team also ended when he was forced to retire from his job.

Bud's professional baseball dreams had ended on a military base, and George no longer had access to the teams he had created, but Maybelle's career was just beginning. The offseason that she and Swannie spent working out with the AAGPBL put Maybelle in the sights of league scouts. In 1948, Maybelle was headed back to Chicago, but this time as a member of the AAGPBL.

3

MAKING IT TO THE PROS

I put on those cleats and as soon as I heard that clickety clack
on the concrete, I thought to myself, "Maybelle, you've made
it. You're a professional baseball player."[1]

By 1947, 20-year-old Maybelle Blair had been playing professional and
recreational softball for years. But she still had not achieved the dream of
playing baseball that went back to her childhood and the Blair family team.
Over the following few years, Blair's life took two dramatic turns: she was
recruited by the AAGPBL to play professional baseball, and she met the
love of her life.

Maybelle spent 1947 in Chicago, playing professional softball for the
Cardinals. When a scout for the AAGPBL approached her about playing
for the league, she was not at all sure she wanted to switch leagues. "Yeah,
I was sitting on the bench with my friends, showing off, throwing curve-
balls, and somebody from the All Americans saw me and said, 'Hey, why
don't you come play baseball?'" Maybelle recalled being quite happy where
she was and saying, "No, no, no. I want to stay here and play." Maybelle
remembered, "I had it made with my girlfriends. I was finally able to be
myself, and I didn't want to give that up." Blair left Chicago at the end
of the 1947 season, confident that she would return as a Chicago Cardinal
the next season.

While back home in California for the summer, Maybelle was again
approached by an official AAGPBL scout, this time at a local ballpark near
where her parents lived in Redondo Beach. Because she had gotten to
know more of the AAGPBL girls while in Chicago, this time she listened
to the offer. Still, she told him she was sure her mother wouldn't let her
go play for this league she had never heard of before. The AAGPBL had

been in existence for five years at that point, and Maybelle was familiar with it, mostly from the women she ran around with. But her parents were not, and even Blair did not know much about the league or those who ran it. She only knew that some of her friends played for the league and that was enough. Blair remembers saying to the scout, "I told you; my mother won't let me leave the house." But he insisted, "Well, I'm going to follow you home anyway. And I'm going to explain to her that I want to hire you." As Maybelle predicted, her mother said, "No, there's no way my daughter's leaving this house." "Well, Mrs. Blair," he said, "you don't understand, we're going to pay her $55 a week." The amount was more money than her father made, so Blair's mother said, "George, go crank up the car. I'm packing her suitcase. She's on the next train out of here." And she was.

As that train rolled into the Chicago train station in May 1948, Blair was excited, but "not as nervous as some of the other girls." Most of the other would-be baseball players had never been to Chicago, and it showed, according to Blair. "Some of the girls were just a little bit overwhelmed, and it may have made it hard for them," Blair said. Even seventy-five years later, the Maybelle Blair bravado showed as she told this story. "Oh, I was excited, but because I had played for the Cardinals and because some of their [AAGPBL] coaches had already seen me pitch, I wasn't too worried." In reality, though, she was afraid of one thing—not about making the team, but about leaving the Cardinals and about the AAGPBL finding out she could barely run. Blair had suffered almost debilitating leg cramps and pulled muscles, and the Cardinal coaches had benched her because of it. She was sure that her strong arm and pitching ability would cover any problems with her legs, and she was right—for a while. After a successful tryout, and, as she had dreamed years before back on that makeshift, dusty baseball field, Maybelle became a professional baseball player with the Peoria Redwings, an AAGPBL expansion team.

The creation of that expansion team spoke to the success of the AAGPBL. The All-American Girls Professional Baseball League was created in 1943 as the All-American Girls Softball League. Philip Wrigley, owner of the Chicago Cubs, asked his general manager, Ken Sells, to find new ways of maintaining the attendance levels at both minor- and major-league ballparks during the war. Aware of the success of women's softball throughout the Midwest, Sells suggested that the creation of a women's professional softball league might help to offset the loss of revenue. Wrigley agreed, and, along with Branch Rickey and Paul V. Harper, he established the All-American Girls Professional Softball League. The league began as a softball league but eventually transitioned to playing baseball. Over the first few years, the basepaths got longer, and pitchers moved from underhanded to strictly overhand pitching. Wrigley sent baseball scouts to amateur and semiprofessional baseball and softball teams around the United States and Canada, looking for talented female players. The scouts held regional try-outs, and, if players made the cut, they were invited to attend the league's final tryouts in Chicago. In April 1943, seventy-five women from the United States and Canada arrived at Wrigley Field. Managers of each team were told to pick seventeen players to start and that, by the time the first spring training was over, each team would be cut to fifteen players. League play began on May 30, 1943, with four teams: the Rockford Peaches, the South Bend Blue Sox, the Kenosha Comets, and the Racine Belles. South Bend played in Rockford, and Kenosha played in Racine.[2]

The popularity of the league grew beyond anything Wrigley could have imagined. The teams were well received by fans in the four home cities, and attendance reached 176,612 for the 1943 season.[3] Because many of the previous attempts to put women on the baseball field had been made by promoters who wanted to make money off the spectacle, the quality of play had not always been good. Fans of the new league were amazed at how well the women played baseball. Enthusiasm and support for the teams spread beyond the original host cities, and the league expanded.[4]

By the time Maybelle joined the league in 1948, the Redwings had been playing for two years. The Peoria Redwings joined the AAGPBL in the 1946 season and remained in the league through 1951. The Redwings had a rocky start in their first season, ending up with a 33–79 record and a disappointing 41 games out of first place in the league's Western Division. The team improved the next season but still did not reach .500. The Redwings' most productive season was in 1948, the year Blair played for them. They finished 71–55 for third place in the division and fourth over-all. Peoria earned a place in the playoffs that year, but they were swept by the Racine Belles in three straight games. Returning to their previous level of play, the Redwings fell to 36–43 and last place in 1949. In 1950, the team finished next to last in the league, and, in 1951, their last season, the team had another losing season, 48-56-2. In six years, they finished over .500 only once. Although the Redwings were not successful, the long-term impact of playing professional baseball was just as great on Redwing players as it was on other All-Americans. Despite the team's record, playing with the AAGPBL was a life-altering experience for Blair. Even after seventy-five years, the friendships, the travel, the baseball, and the fun remain emblazoned on her memory.

When Maybelle is asked about her playing days, she often relies on one particular story, a tale about playing in dresses. "We played in those dresses, which wasn't a problem, except we didn't have sliding pants like you all do today. We slid on bare legs. I'm still picking gravel out of my rear end." This well-told story still gets a laugh. Maybelle keeps telling it for that reason, and because, while it is about playing baseball, it is the humor, not the act of playing, that is the focus. Similarly, for Blair, playing in the AAGPBL mattered a great deal, but what mattered most did not happen on the field. The most significant memories are those centered around the people, the friendships, and the fun.

During her time with the Redwings, Maybelle made good friends. Some were teammates, and others were local fans. For a reason Maybelle cannot recall, three younger girls who were fans latched onto her. They followed her around, and when she came down with a terrible toothache that summer the girls went to a pharmacy and bought her medicine. Even when she was moved from one residence to another, they followed her. On more than one occasion they showed up to do her laundry, Blair remembered. It was common for local fans to support the teams or even pick favorite players to follow, but that level of fandom was extreme. "Today people might say they were stalkers, but I didn't mind. They were harmless and friendly. Truthfully, I liked the attention." It wasn't just Peoria where the AAGPBL players were idolized. In every town with an AAGPBL team, players were respected and often seen as local heroes. For many players, it was the first time they had been noticed and even celebrated for playing ball, a feeling not lost on Blair. "I was always a showoff. You know, an entertainer. Even as a little kid. But when I got attention for playing ball, that was different. Now that made me proud."

Being proud and even having a small band of groupies following them around did not stop Blair or the rest of the players from having a good time. "Lord, could I tell you some stories," Blair said with a laugh. "Some things may not seem funny to anyone else, or mild compared to today, but we thought we had invented fun." And mischief. Many of Blair's stories from playing in the AAGPBL are full of mischievousness. When Blair moved in with Gloria Ruiz, one of the league's Cuban ballplayers, it seemed they encouraged one another. The AAGPBL had strict beauty requirements. Players could not have short hair; they had to wear makeup and always represent the league by maintaining the highest contemporary standards of femininity. Ruiz was an attractive young woman who adhered to the league rules about beauty standards. For some reason, though, she decided she wanted to be a blonde. It took little to convince Maybelle and her friend Faye Dancer to dye Gloria's hair. "We didn't know what we were doing," Blair said. "We'd never dyed anyone's hair before but off we went to the drug store. By the time we were done she had the ugliest red hair you've ever seen." Retelling this story left Blair in stitches, pausing every few words to catch her breath from laughing. They all got in trouble and were fined by the league. Maybelle has no idea what the fine was, but, whatever it was, it was well worth the laughter it brought her later.

Gloria Ruiz was present in a number of Blair's league stories. In fact, she instigated some of them. By the time Maybelle began playing for Peoria, she had a car. Most of the women did not, and so she was both envied and pestered by the other players. Blair remembered that one day Gloria decided that she did not want to wait on Blair or anyone else to drive her; she would do it herself. "She'd never driven a car in her life. She grabbed my keys and ran out the door, me hot on her tail. I jumped in the passenger's side just as she took off like a bat out of hell. We almost had a wreck. I thought she was going to kill us both. Once we stopped, she just got out. Didn't say anything. Just got out." Fortunately, Gloria did not terrorize Peoria with her driving again, but that car figures into many more stories from Maybelle's year as an All-American.

Another incident involved Twila Shively, an outfielder for the Red Wings and a good friend of both Blair's and Faye Dancer's. Shively broke her leg while sliding into second base and had to be hospitalized. In the 1940s, patients spent several days in the hospital for such injuries. Because visiting hours were strict and because their practice and game schedules were full, Maybelle and Faye weren't able to visit Twila. After a few days, both became determined to see her. They found black sheets or a large cloth of some kind and drove to the hospital in Blair's car. "We pulled my car up to the fire escape then put those black sheets over us and up we went. From the top of my car to the fire escape, then we climbed through Twi's window. We almost scared her to death. Nearly killed all of us but Faye and I saw her."

Many of Blair's AAGPBL stories involved Faye Dancer, one of the league's most popular and beloved players. She helped dye Gloria's hair, snuck into the hospital, and, according to Blair, stored beer in the pockets of her large coat so they could drink while traveling on the bus. In hindsight, it is the stories of friends, shenanigans, and simply being part of a team that most stand out about Maybelle's time in the league.

Although she was invited back the next year, Maybelle's professional baseball experience with the Redwings was limited to just that one season. "They loved my pitching, but then they realized I couldn't move off the mound, so I didn't play much. At the end of the season, though, [league manager] Max Carey gave me a contract. It was blank with his name on it. And he wanted me back in '49 because he loved my arm." Maybelle considered going back to the league in 1949, but she also knew that she was not likely to play a lot. Despite ending her dream of playing professional baseball, she decided to move on from the AAGPBL.

Blair would be the first to admit that she was not a superstar in the AAGPBL. Like every other former player, though, she is proud of her time in the league and her place in the history of women's baseball in the United States. Injured legs may have limited her time on the field, but they did not keep her from having fun, making lifelong friends, and "just being myself." It was the independence she experienced while playing ball and the reaffirmation of her sense of self she acquired alongside her teammates that gave Blair confidence and that were, in hindsight, the most significant aspects of her time in the league. It took her years to recognize what really mattered about playing with the AAGPBL. "I did not realize it at the time," Maybelle said. "But being part of that group, that league left a mark. I guess you could say I was proud of being an All-American. That gave me some confidence to do other things, I think."

At the end of the 1948 season, Maybelle realized her time in the league was limited. "By this time, it was clear I wasn't ever going to get married, so I decided I had to do something to earn a living." This was a familiar refrain among the former AAGPBL players. While many did get married and have families, several did not. Growing up during the Great Depression instilled a visceral understanding about poverty and the importance of work and making money. Like many of her teammates, rather than return to Peoria in 1949, Maybelle went back home in search of a career, a permanent job, and a life outside of baseball and softball. Not "without baseball and softball," she reminded me.

4

LOVE AND LOSS

Upon returning home to the Los Angeles area, Maybelle entered the Los Angeles School of Physiotherapy. "School was never a big, important deal to me, and I never thought I would go beyond high school, but I had to do something, and I saw how physiotherapists worked when I played ball. So, I applied and got in." Without even realizing it at the time, Blair relied on that newfound confidence when she embarked on a whole new life. After graduation she began work for a Dr. Boonshaft in Hollywood, treating patients with multiple sclerosis. Despite having a well-paying job, Maybelle was back home living with her parents. It was her mother who would later insist that Blair leave that job.

Maybelle loved the work but, by her own admission, she got too involved in it. "I loved all of my patients. You could just see them deteriorating. They would look at me with hope in their eyes, you know, and I try to encourage them. It took a toll." Too much of one according to her mother, so Blair quit. Because of the stress she had begun losing weight, and her mother was convinced that the job was the reason, so she insisted that Maybelle leave. "My mother made me quit because I lost all my weight. I went down from a hundred, and she says, baby, you got to quit." Iva Blair was the boss, so, after a year, Maybelle left her position with Dr. Boonshaft and began doing massage work at home. Blair was squeamish about touching male bodies, and, when a man got sexually aroused during a massage, she threw up her hands and walked away—away from him and from that job. After quitting the massage business, Maybelle fell back on a familiar and comfortable job. She went back to working at Northrop Airlines on a part-time basis. Settled in a place where she felt safe, Maybelle was happy. She still had softball, her friends, and a sense of adventure.

31

While playing softball on local recreational teams, Blair was noticed by the coaches of the New Orleans Jax, a professional women's softball team. In the 1940s, the Jax Girls, a women's softball team originally comprised of Jax Brewing employees, was extremely popular and very successful. Known as one of the best women's softball teams in the country, the Jax drew huge crowds wherever they played, from California to Chicago to Canada. "Anyone who knew softball knew about the Jax," Blair remembered. They won seven national softball championships between 1942 and 1949 before disbanding.[1] During a swing through California, many of the Jax players became friends with local players, in many cases attending some of the same gay bars. Blair was among the group hanging out with the Jax players, and, when she attended some of the Jax practices, they invited her to play. In the brief time she played second base for them, she traveled to Canada, Oregon, and Seattle. The trips with the team were a wonderful experience for Maybelle. The team paid for the travel and even paid the players. Even though it wasn't a large salary, Blair was grateful to have it as a supplement to her part-time work at Northrop Aircraft. The team was even planning to go overseas to play for the troops, but the sponsors decided it was too dangerous. Still, this period was important to Blair's personal development as well as to her growth as a ballplayer.

One of Maybelle's best memories of her time with the Jax was a trip to Bakersfield, California, where the team played against the men's world champion softball team:

> Here's what happened. Our pitcher, Ronnie Jackson, was as tall as this building and had arms about as long as Satchel Paige's. She pitched from our distance, shorter than the men's, and the men had to pitch from theirs. Well, they couldn't hit her, and we couldn't touch him either. Somehow, I got on base, a walk. Somehow, I think, I got to third base. Rita called time and came over to me and said, "Pretend you're injured. I'm gonna run for you." I said okay, so I got to aching and carrying on. They took me out, and she took my place. She had noticed that when the catcher got the ball he'd walk halfway to the pitcher before throwing it underhand to him. So, she wandered down a little way from the base and then, when he flipped the ball, she took off like a bat out of hell and scored the run. Slid right underneath. He was not alert and never thought a girl could do this to a man. We beat them one to nothing.

According to Maybelle, all those women were baseball and softball savvy. They knew a lot about playing but also about strategy. Blair remembers using much of what she learned from her time with the Jax on other teams. Maybelle only played with the Jax for a short time, mostly during their West Coast tour, but she still maintains that that team was among the absolute best she ever saw or played with.

Never far from a diamond, after leaving the Jax, Maybelle continued to play softball with the Pasadena Ramblers, the team she had played with during the war. She also continued to work part time at Northrop Aircraft. There, Blair found an admirer and ally in Jack Northrop. "He would come in all the time, so I got to know him. He was the greatest guy, honest to God. Every time I think of him it brings tears to my eyes because everyone loved him so. That's why working at Northrop was so great. If I had to go back and do it again, that's exactly what I'd want to do, work at Northrop. Mr. Northrop ran his company first class. Everybody was family. At one time, I think he knew everybody by name." One summer, when Blair was about twenty-two years old and working in the mailroom, her manager, impressed with her work ethic, asked if she would be interested in a full-time job in transportation. "I jumped at the chance," Blair said. "I first became a courier for one year."

Once hired for full-time work at Northrop, Maybelle did what she always did—she created a place for women to play ball. "I put together a softball team there at Northrop. I worked 'em hard and we were pretty darn good. In fact, Mr. Northrop himself would come out and say, 'Boy, you sure are throwing good today, Maybelle.'" Blair's softball team played around the area against other companies and sometimes against men's teams within Northrop. Jack Northrop was a fan of Maybelle's softball-playing skills, but he saw her ingenuity and determination as an asset as well. She literally worked her way from the mailroom to management—probably just what Jack Northrop imagined she would do.

Working as a courier gave Maybelle an opportunity to meet and learn from a lot of people. At first, Maybelle thought her job as a courier wasn't that important. Once she started naming the people she drove around, she changed her mind. "I picked up small parcels or delivered packages or mail, anything. Oh, and I also went and picked up VIPs." Among those she transported was Brigadier General Ennis Whitehead, Commander of the Fifth Air Force of the United States Pacific Air Forces. The general was fond of Maybelle. According to her, he was a bit too fond. "My God, he called me at my house and wanted to go out with me. I was so scared, so I had my mother lie for me, tell him I wasn't home." In addition to the generals, Maybelle drove other high-ranking military personnel. She was asked to pick up a high-ranking military doctor. Blair does not remember his name, but he was the doctor to the head of Northrop Aircraft at the time, Thomas V. Jones. "Can you believe that?" she said. "I went to our president's house and had lunch with him and this doctor. They wouldn't have me sit out in the car, so they invited me in to have lunch at his home. Mr. Jones was something else." Jones had a very different personality from Jack Northrop's. He was flashier and had a fondness for the finer things, according to Blair. Jones was known for socializing with European royalty and befriended the Shah of Iran. While president of Northrop, he hosted elaborate parties that included foreign dignitaries and politically powerful individuals, such as his friend Ronald Reagan and the widow of Chiang Kai-shek.[2] Despite Jones's penchant for fancy things and the company of famous people, to Blair he remains the man who invited her into his house rather than leave her sitting alone in a car.

Maybelle's experiences as a courier also put her in a car with Daniel "Chappie" James. As a member of the famed Tuskegee Airmen, James served as a trainer during World War II and fought in Korea and Vietnam. He became the first African American to attain the rank of four-star general and later became vice commander of the 33rd Tactical Fighter Wing at Eglin Air Force Base. "Meeting him was exciting, but one of my favorite memories is when I drove Ronald Reagan. It was before he was president of course, but I drove him around. What a nice man he was." Maybelle had exciting experiences as a courier and loved the job. Laughing, she said, "I think I was good at it because I like to talk, to entertain." Her supervisors noticed how she handled the job and the quirks of all those VIPs. Within a year, they asked her to become a dispatcher. In retrospect, Blair is clear that she was merely a spectator in the lives of all those famous people, but she remains proud of how she represented Northrop Aircraft and happy that she got to have so much fun. "I loved that job," she said. "I got to know the guys in transportation very well so becoming a dispatcher was a natural progression. I was good at talking and even better at telling people where to go, so I got the job."

Maybelle was a dispatcher for two years. During that period, she continued to impress her bosses. She also continued to play softball and, as she emphatically points out, "have a whole lot of fun." Her recollections of that time are full of tales of softball games and stories about the women she met, where she met them, and their adventures.

After spending time on her own in Chicago and traveling with the Ramblers and the Jax, Maybelle was more comfortable in her own skin and much more willing to frequent some of the gay bars the Los Angeles area had to offer. One of Blair's favorites was the IF Club, the first gay bar that she had visited in Los Angeles. As most LGBT people did in the 1940s and

1950s, Maybelle knew the risks of being caught at a gay bar. She could lose her job and even her freedom if there was a raid. During this period, gay men were more likely to be targeted by police, who used decoys to entrap them. In general, lesbians did not face similar aggressive, entrapment tactics, but they knew to stay hidden. If found wearing "masculine-looking" clothes, frequenting gay bars, or "being visibly homosexual," they faced arrest and prison in the state of California. Thinking back to that time, Maybelle said, "I was aware that I had a lot more to lose. I was scared to death of being found out and what that would do to my family and to Northrop, so I was careful." Scary as it was, that fear did not stop Maybelle from having a good time, "in or out of the bars"—even after she and her friends were in a raid themselves.

In and around the Los Angeles area, there were frequent bar raids, close calls, and arrests throughout the 1940s and 1950s. Bars for women were raided and, according to witnesses, even though women were usually arrested on trumped-up charges, police were often brutal during these raids. The transcript of one court case from 1959 listed the charges as "serving liquor to an intoxicated person."[3] The alcohol was allegedly bought by a woman who was dressed in male clothing and put her arm around the body of another female.[4] The arrest was made by an undercover officer. Transcripts rarely described the injuries of those arrested. That information had to come from the women themselves and, according to those willing to talk about the experience, the raids were terrifying. Police were brutal and often employed what many referred to as "Gestapo tactics."[5]

Intellectually, knowing that arrest and public shame were possible is one thing. Really thinking it can happen to you is another. "On one hand you know it, but on the other, you think, nah, I'm faster, smarter than they are. I'm fine," Blair said, as she launched into the story of her own frightening raid experience.

As they had done many times, Maybelle, her lifelong friend Jean Reed, Tiby Eisen, and a girlfriend of Tiby's were all at a bar along the Santa Monica pier. Maybelle remembers,

> We were in there, you know, drinking and having a good time, danc-
> ing, and carrying on. Mostly carrying on. And all of a sudden, somebody
> yells, "Raid!" That's how everybody warned each other. Called out,
> "It's a raid." Girls were scared to death, running every direction. We
> had all come in Jean's old car. That silly thing we had to push it half the
> time just to get it started. But that night it started. She [Jean] had gone
> outside as soon as she heard the call, and each of us walked out some

open windows, and there she was in that car. She hauled us all out of there. None of us got caught but there was a big article in the paper the next day. We were so lucky.

They *were* lucky. Jean was a schoolteacher, Maybelle was employed at Northrop, and Tiby worked for the Stratham Instrument Company. All of them would have been fired had they been caught up in the raid, and, as Blair added, "Our lives would have been over." While that statement may sound overly dramatic to some, to Maybelle and her friends in the mid-twentieth century, it felt like truth.

In a world where just being herself was dangerous, it was not easy for Blair to balance her job at Northrop, playing softball, and her personal life. "I was scared to death all the time that people would find out and I would lose my job at Northrop," she recalled. They didn't find out or, if they did, they didn't care as much as Maybelle feared. Her bosses continued to promote her, and after only two years as a courier she was asked to move into management. The bosses "wanted me to become a supervisor in transportation," Blair remembered, "but I didn't know much about the trucks or other vehicles so I told them that I would only do it if they would teach me to drive every vehicle we had." For months, Blair spent time on the night shift, learning to drive every vehicle in the department. Employing the same level of dedication and determination she previously used to create baseball and softball opportunities, Maybelle built a strong department and a successful career.

When Maybelle became the manager of the transportation department, she was one of only three female managers in the company. She simply did not pay attention to things like that, however. "At that time, I didn't think about being a woman in the job. I was just doing my job, and I loved every minute. Northrop was the best company in the whole cockeyed world. They opened the doors for so many people, not only for women." Maybelle graciously gives the company and her crew credit for her success. "They [Northrop] gave more opportunities to employees. I was very fortunate working for Northrop. I never felt like the only girl; everyone treated me with respect. We had such a great crew that it was a piece of cake for me." In reality, though, Maybelle used her baseball foundation to put together a great department.

Blair knew that teams are only as strong as their individual teammates, so she set out to build a strong transportation department team. "When I interviewed new candidates, they had to like baseball or I wouldn't hire them," she said with a laugh. "Honestly, it was any sport." In her experience, if a potential employee had played sports of any kind, they would likely be a good fit for the transportation department. "I could tell the athletes when they walked in the door. How they walked, the confidence. Those guys made good drivers." Northrop's confidence in Blair paid off. Her department was well run and successful. Even though she may not have purposefully set out to become a role model for other women in the company, that is exactly what she did. Recently, Maybelle Blair was interviewed by a young woman whose father was hired by Blair in the 1960s. Following in her father's footsteps, the young woman is now employed at Northrop. When she got the job, her father said, "there was this woman who hired me. Maybelle Blair. She opened your door. You do the same for someone else." In retelling that story, Blair still gave the credit to Northrop. "Mr. Northrop's dedication to his employees fostered loyalty among us too. I wanted to do my best for him because he was the one who opened the door for me, but, in the meantime, I guess I did open some doors, too." She did, and for herself as well.

As Blair moved up the ranks within Northrop, her salary and her business opportunities grew, and she took advantage of them. Once she moved into management, most of her time was spent working, she remembered. "I was dedicated to my job and to my guys. We had the best department in the whole company. Now, that did not stop me from having a good time. You know what they say, though, 'work hard, play hard.'" She said with a laugh, "I did both." There were parties, nights at local bars, and "a number of you know, episodes, with some of the girls." In Blair lingo and in the coded language of the time, an "episode" means a sexual relationship. "God, we had fun, well, I did anyway." Claiming to be too busy for a serious relationship, Blair talked about all her sexual encounters.

While she was focused on work in this period of her life, many of the women Maybelle dated during the early 1950s were connected in some way to softball or baseball. "You see, I wasn't all that serious at that time. About relationships, I mean. There were crushes and stuff, but then there were some of the girls who were after me too. You remember Snookie, right? Well, we had an episode. She was always after me." Her "episode" with Snookie lasted a year, on and off, she said. "We never lived together or anything. She was married at the time." Eventually Snookie got divorced, but, despite having an opportunity to rekindle their relationship, Maybelle and Snookie remained only friends until Snookie's death in 2011.

The 1950s were an exciting, sometimes scary, and often wonderful decade in Maybelle's life. She had financial independence and an active social life, and, in 1955, she met her match, the woman she still calls "the love of her life."

In 1955, Blair bought a house, her first, in Torrence, California. "I was so darn proud of that house," she remembered. "A lot of the girls had parties back then and now that I had a house I could too. So, I did, and boy did we have fun." At one of those parties, Maybelle met a woman named Jenai Forbes, who was at the time going with Blair's friend, Shirley Mehaffey. Blair and Shirley had been friends for a long time and even had an episode of their own at one point. Shirley even accompanied Maybelle on Sundays when she took her nephew, Rod, for the day, which she did every week. Sometimes they went to the zoo and, other times, to a ball game, the beach, or horse races. Blair was dedicated to Rod and even helped coach him once he started playing Little League baseball. If Mehaffey wanted to spend time with Maybelle on a Sunday, it was going to include Rod. So, despite recognizing a quickly developing attraction between Jenai and herself, Maybelle respected that friendship.

For a year Maybelle and Jenai spent time together, ran in the same circles, played golf, and got to know one another better. Blair remembers that Jenai was close to perfect. She was beautiful, athletic, and smart. Soon, Blair recalled that "the writing was on the wall. Eventually we got together and about a year later she moved in with me. I thought that was my 'happily ever after.'" Life was about as good as Blair could have imagined. She continued to work in management at Northrop. Jenai was a banker at Security Bank so together they were financially secure. And, as Blair made clear, they were in love.

Since Jenai's mother had died when she was a baby, she was raised by her father. Jenai and her father were never close, and Blair remembered him as, "no good. An idiot." She recalled, "Not counting him, which you shouldn't, she didn't have family. But she sure became part of the Blair family, though." Maybelle's brother, Bud, his wife, Peggy, and their son, Rod, loved Jenai and included her in all family gatherings. Even the weekly racetrack outings. "Every Saturday my brother, me, Jenai, and Rod, he was a little kid, would go to the racetrack. Hollywood Park. We had season tickets, and all of us loved the races. Including Jenai." Whether it was horse racing, family celebrations, or holidays, Jenai and Maybelle were there as family, at least in their hearts. Blair never discussed her sexuality with Bud or Peggy, so she and Jenai were not open about their relationship. In every way that mattered, though, they were family.

Jenai also became part of the Sunday outings with Blair and Rod. Blair "never missed a Sunday or a chance to play ball with that kid." Bud managed Rod's Little League team and, Blair was quick to add, "coached him up a bit. You know, practice hitting and throwing. That kid started playing almost as soon as he could walk." Rod was a good ballplayer, and a great shortstop, as Blair remembered. He played through all the divisions of Little League and even into high school, but "he just never grew." Rod's memories of those days with the woman he called simply "Aunt" were as vibrant and happy as were Blair's. "It was always a great time for me," Rod said. "It was never like I had to go and didn't want to. Most of our outings involved baseball. Not all, sometimes we went to the zoo and later to the horse races, but early on it was mostly baseball."[6] Some of Rod's earliest memories were of going to see the Los Angeles Angels play at "little" Wrigley Field. At that time, the Angles were an AAA team for the Cubs. As a nod to the Chicago Cubs, the field where they played was named after the famed Wrigley Field in Chicago. Rod remembered that those games were before 1958 when the Dodgers moved to Los Angeles from Brooklyn. "I remember I could hardly wait to get there. That was a gift. I mean, this was not a boring day for me."[7]

There were occasional mishaps, like Rod getting lost at an Angels game and ending up at the very top of Wrigley Field, or when he got in trouble with his dad and then his teacher for telling his entire third-grade class that his aunt was taking him to the Dodgers opening-day game during school hours. "That was a big day. We weren't going to miss it. Sometimes my dad and Jenai would go places with us. Not this time. It was just Aunt and me. I remember where we sat at the Coliseum. Going there for the Dodgers first ever game in LA with Aunt is one of my best memories."[8]

Not all their outings together were at ballparks. Some took place at the Orpheum Theater in Los Angeles. "I think she liked to go to the Orpheum, which was a very ornate theater house in downtown LA. She took me a few times. Always her choice of movies and I'm not sure what she was thinking sometimes. We saw [*The Wreck of*] *Mary Deare*. I think Gary Cooper was probably one of her favorites. Then, later we saw the *Judgment at Nuremberg*. They probably would not have been my choices, but she said, 'let's go,' so I did."[9] Regardless of where they went, for many years Jenai went along, solidifying Maybelle and Rod's relationship and Jenai's role in the Blair family.

When Northrop transferred Bud to South Dakota in 1960, he, Peggy, and Rod moved away. The loss of regular contact with her brother and his family was difficult for Blair. As Rod remembered, though, "Aunt and Jenai drove all the way to South Dakota together to see us and to watch me play ball. We lived kind of out in the sticks, and people couldn't always find us so, when we knew they were expected, my dad and I got in the car and drove up to the road to where they would be coming in and waited. We hadn't been there long when we looked to the right at a little rise in the road and there was a little brown Nash Rambler cresting the hill. It looked like Bullitt in that movie. All four tires were off the ground as she came flying over that hill and right past us doing about eighty. Dad said, 'Well, there she goes.'" Once they got Blair and Jenai to the house, Rod remembered that it was a great visit and one during which they all got to know Jenai better and love her even more. "After all, not everyone could ride in a car with Aunt for that long."[10]

Just over a year later, when Rod and his family returned to California from South Dakota, Blair and Jenai returned to weekly visits and outings with Rod. Rod remembered that it was about that time that they "bought that beauty shop. I didn't know what they were doing but I think it was successful. You know Aunt. She is good at everything. Even business."[11] Maybelle was known as the member of the family who could and did try anything. She was adventuresome and brave, Rod remembered. "I was never surprised by what she did next."[12]

Both Blair and Jenai had a lot of business sense, so, after a few years together, they decided to find some kind of business to buy. "We wanted to have a business of our own and, really, we didn't know what kind it would be. Then we found this little beauty shop for sale. And it looked like a nice little business to run so we bought it." Two sisters owned the shop, but they had decided to retire and were selling the shop fully equipped. When Blair heard about the opportunity, she discussed it with Jenai, and together they bought the Beauty Shop, around 1961.

When Maybelle and Jenai took over the shop, the first thing Blair did was to go next door to the liquor store and buy champagne. No matter the time of their appointment on Saturdays, each woman got a glass of champagne. "God, they loved coming in. It didn't take long before all six of my operators were booked solid every weekend." Unsurprisingly, many of those clients became weekly customers. Maybelle fondly remembered a Japanese woman who quickly became one of her most dedicated customers:

> She hadn't been here too long and didn't speak much English. She came in one day and said, "I need to get my hair done." We worked her in. I knew it was going to be a wait, so I sat her down and asked if she'd like a little champagne. She said, "Ohh, I like champagne." Before she left, she was half snookered. She got her hair done, and before she left she promised she'd be back next week. Sure enough, the next Saturday she

was there, laughing. "When I got home last week, my husband asked, 'Where have you been?'" She said, "I've been at the beauty shop. He did not believe it and told me I had to confess. So, I confess that I am in the beauty shop I love."

That woman was one of many who became loyal customers of the Beauty Shop. "It's amazing what just a little bit of champagne will do. My customers had nothing but fun, and, when you are having fun someplace, you are coming back." Maybelle was a master at fun and at keeping her customers happy, which is why Jenai called her the shop socializer.

After work at Northrop and every Saturday, Maybelle was there at the shop, working as the receptionist and socializing. If any of the hairdressers were running behind, Maybelle would help out by "testing their curls or to see if they were dry, then I'd say 'Oh I think you need ten more minutes. You want some more champagne?' 'Yes, Maybelle I will have a little more.' That way they didn't get anxious or mind if we were running late." The Beauty Shop was always a fun and festive place to work and to have your hair done. Every holiday, especially Halloween, all the hairdressers, Blair, and even customers dressed up. They made every client's experience a party.

While Blair socialized, Jenai took care of the financial end of the business, what Blair remembers as "the hard stuff." "All I did was come in after work and I worked Saturdays. On the weekend she [Jenai] stayed home and took care of the house. Yeah, she took care of the lawn. She did everything while I worked. She says it's more important for you to be down there socializing. So, I did." In addition to being a fun place, the Beauty Shop was also a financial success. After only a couple of years, Maybelle and Jenai talked about opening another shop with a long-term goal of having three shops. That did not happen, however, and neither did Blair's happily ever after.

As they had always done, Blair and Jenai not only worked hard but also played hard. Both were members of a golf club and played every Sunday. Jenai was very good, Blair remembered. "We had so much fun. We'd play golf, go to the bar, and laugh and have so much fun." In 1971, Jenai won a spot in a tournament playoff, and "this one Sunday we were going to the Valley for her to have that playoff. The winner would be the champion. She wasn't feeling well that morning, and I told her we needed to stay home." Jenai had asthma and thought nothing about her breathing problems that morning. Maybelle and Jenai headed off to the tournament finals and had gone roughly twenty miles when Jenai said, "Maybelle, I can't breathe." Maybelle said, "Oh my God. I gotta turn this car around and go home." Jenai agreed, but on the trip home her breathing worsened. So, Blair went directly to Hawthorne Hospital. After about an hour, Jenai emerged with a prescription and a diagnosis of a simple asthma attack. Both women were relieved and went home, where Blair insisted Jenai rest while she went to the shop to do the laundry. The laundromat was next door, so Blair loaded up the towels and put them in the machines. Within a few minutes, someone came in to tell her that the phone was ringing in the shop. "Thank God, I ran over there and answered. It was Jenai." When Jenai told Maybelle she couldn't breathe, Maybelle recalls,

> I left everything then leaped into my car. By the time I got home she was in bad shape. I got her in the car and there was a fire station about half a block away from my house. I picked her up, drove her down there. She fell on the floor at the fire station. They sort of gave her some oxygen, and the ambulance came. I leaped into it with them. By the time we got to the hospital, they were doing that tracheotomy thing. She never woke up. It turns out she had pneumonia. They wanted me to pull the plug on her. And I said, "Don't die and we gonna try and try and try." I think I held out for about three or four days. The doctors and nurses said, "Maybelle, she's brain dead. You're just keeping the body alive." I just couldn't do it. Then, my brother says, "Sis. I understand what you're going through, but you gotta do it." So, I had to pull the plug on her.

Jenai died on June 8, 1971, at the age of forty. Her family, Maybelle, Bud, and Peggy were all there at the end. "I couldn't really tell anyone, or most people, how much of a loss this was. I think Bud and Peggy knew. They knew. God, I was devastated. Absolutely devastated."

Bud, Peggy, and Rod were devastated, too. Rod recalled, "We love[d] Jenai. All of us. We started to go to Jenai and Aunt's house on Christmas Eve, They, mostly Jenai I believe, would make this gourmet Christmas Eve dinner. We had steak and lots of other things. We always had a wonderful dinner at their house. That went on until Jenai died. Such an awful thing. Sudden. I was young but I remember how all of us missed her. Especially Aunt."[13]

Maybelle, just forty-four years old, was at a loss. "I could hardly stand it. Here we had the shop, this whole future, and it was gone. I had employees that needed me to keep the shop, so I did, for about a year anyway." Blair received as much loyalty as she gave at Northrop, so, after Jenai's death, the woman who was her boss's secretary stepped in to help her with the shop's finances. Blair would gather the information, and her friend would come to her house and spend the night and they would do payroll for the shop. "She was married and had twins. I think she just wanted to get away from them, honestly. We would drink, get drunk, and have a ball. It's a wonder my employees ever got paid. She didn't know I was gay. God, no clue. She felt sorry for me, I think, that Jenai died. Nothing ever happened between us. She was just a very good friend." Even with help, it became increasingly difficult for Maybelle to keep the shop open, so, just under a year after Jenai died, she sold the Beauty Shop.

From the day Maybelle heard the "clickety clack" of those cleats on the Peoria Redwing pavement, she thought her life was full, complete. She was playing professional ball, making good money, owned a car, and was, by her own admission, "having a great time." She was young and never thought life would be better or worse than it was at that moment. It did not take long for reality to break through. "Just when you think you have it figured out," Blair recalled, "Life goes sideways, and you have to rethink. Too bad we don't realize that when we are young." After only one year in Peoria, her legs were in such bad shape that Maybelle had to leave the league. She returned to California to find work and continued to play softball when she could. Along the way she found a career at Northrop and met the love of her life, Jenai Forbes. As it had been in the 1940s, the happy, content life Blair had created for herself was shattered when Jenai died suddenly in 1971. Once again it was time to move beyond what was supposed to happen and create a new plan for the future.

5

RETIREMENT?

I retired from my job, but not baseball. Never from baseball![1]

From the time she was a small child, Blair usually had a plan: a plan for the next baseball game or field, a plan for the next business deal or house to buy, and even a plan for the next romantic interest. That level of focus, and her life's compass, was lost when Jenai died in 1971. Maybelle was "for the first time, unsure what to do. I didn't have her, and I was just lost. Nothing to keep me grounded." Not even baseball. Without realizing it, during her relationship with Jenai, Blair had gotten away from the hands-on connection to baseball that had sustained her for years. Softball and baseball were present, but only peripherally. "I got away from it a bit," she remembered. "I played with my nephew and continued to be a fan, but that was about it." The focus of Maybelle's life with Jenai was not baseball, but to survive her loss Maybelle would rely on the game and the teammates she loved.

Despite the pain of losing Jenai, "I never just laid down and died," Blair said. "That's not my personality. I tried to keep going. I worked hard and continued to go out and meet people. You know what I mean." Many of Maybelle's friends had parties, and she went to ball games where a lot of friends from her own playing days either played or watched. She kept her social life full, and friends often tried to fix her up with single women they knew.

Most of those dates did little to penetrate the sadness or distract Maybelle from the heartbreak of losing Jenai. One did. "Of course I got tangled up with my good friend Swannie's girlfriend, Teddy Hamilton," Blair remembered. Teddy and Swannie had been together for what Blair called a "hundred years," so she kept telling Teddy that they could not get involved. Teddy was persistent, and Blair was not as successful at staying away from her as she should have been, so "the back-and-forth" continued. "Teddy started sending me cards. Snoopy cards. About how much she missed me and all of this and that. You know the old routine." Blair admits she did not resist as strongly as she should have at the time. "The company was nice, I guess. It helped me, you know, helped me get through. Although it caused me a lot of problems with Swannie. Teddy kept telling me that she was absolutely through with Swannie. I said, 'Look, Swannie's my friend, Teddy, and I'm not fooling around with you.' It was hard, she was so darling." Teddy was extremely attractive and, as Blair said, "a great softball pitcher. She played for the Lionettes and also for one of the Chicago teams. We had a lot in common."

Blair worked the night shift at Northrop during this time, so Teddy would come to her house and have lunch. "We would play rummy and bet on it. It was fun. Anyway, it turned out we sort of had a little hanky-panky going on, you know?" Maybelle knew she needed to stop seeing Teddy, but Teddy was persistent, and, as she readily admits, she was weak. "She just wouldn't leave me alone. Well, it was me too. She was a beautiful woman." The situation was difficult, and eventually Blair decided that the best solution was to move. She sold her house in Torrence and moved to Rossmore. While only thirty minutes away from Teddy, Maybelle hoped the increased physical distance would help. It did—temporarily. Their connection was never really severed. Teddy and Blair remained friends, and, much later in life, after Swannie passed away, they rekindled their love affair. That too was short lived, but they did remain friends until Teddy's death in 2011.

Despite the losses and the relocation, the one constant in Maybelle's life through the 1970s was her career at Northrop. She continued to impress her superiors, which led to promotions and more responsibility. One of the jobs she is most proud of was coordinating the transportation of planes from Northrop to Edwards Air Force Base. Many of the planes had to be moved overland, and the planning of that task fell to Blair. Her most memorable experience with working in transportation was when she oversaw the movement of a YF-17 fighter aircraft, complete with wings attached. The plane had to be towed from the Los Angeles area to Edwards Air Force Base in the Mojave Desert. Blair had to plan the route first; then coordinate with the fire departments, police, and city engineers; then secure city, state, and federal road permits. Her team practiced, without the plane itself, but nothing prepared her for the actual event.

Getting the plane through downtown Los Angeles was one of the most difficult aspects of the mission. Blair remembered a man staggering out of a downtown bar and looking up at an aircraft wing. "Rather than pink elephants, he saw a fighter plane pass over him," she said. "He stood there for a few seconds and went right back into the bar." The trip was scheduled to last approximately three hours. "We left about midnight and even stopped in front of the LA city hall on the way. Around 3 a.m. we rolled into Edwards." She was never so relieved in her life, "One tiny dent in the aircraft would mean complete failure. When we stopped, I hopped out of the lead truck and my knees buckled. One of my guys had to hold me up. I could barely stand. Even today when I think about that I get nervous. I can't believe we pulled that off," she said with a laugh. "What experiences I've had."

Maybelle's thirty-five-year career at Northrop was full of successes, such as moving planes through major cities. But, as she had always done, Maybelle also found a way to give Northrop women and men a place to play ball. From the creation of the company's first women's softball team in the first years of her employment at Northrop to the development and management of two men's teams in the 1970s, Blair created baseball and softball opportunities for herself and other Northrop employees. But Maybelle's dedication to her career, her work ethic, and all the "time she spent running around, playing" began to take its toll on her health.

In 1980 and into 1981, Maybelle became extremely ill. She was rushed to a hospital where tests showed she had water around her heart. After a tricky surgery, she was kept in a critical care unit for three weeks. Once released from the hospital, Maybelle stayed with her brother, Bud, and his wife, Peggy, who Blair credits with keeping her alive. "I have no idea what I would have done without them. I would have died, I think." Maybelle's condition and subsequent recovery were so serious that she missed three months of work. After the health scare and at the urging of her family, Maybelle, now in her fifties, began thinking about retirement. It took another five years, but in 1986 Blair retired from Northrop. Unsurprisingly, Maybelle claims she did not see leaving Northrop as "real retirement. You know, sitting around and getting old." Rather, it was simply the end of an inning.

After that health scare, as Blair was moving toward retirement from Northrop, she was very much involved with her community of friends and former baseball and softball players. "I was still very social, even as I got older. Looking back, I guess I wasn't that old then, was I?" Maybelle retired at age fifty-nine and never stopped moving. "When they retire, some people just buy a boat and go fishing or play golf every day. I couldn't do that. I only have two speeds. Fast and stopped. I wasn't ready to stop then and I'm still not." After retirement, Maybelle moved again, this time to a large ranch in the mountains, then moved again and bought property in Palm Springs. Together with a new girlfriend, Donna McLain, she ran a branch of Elderhostel in Palm Springs. Her relationship with Donna was the first serious relationship Maybelle had after Jenai's death, but, as she remembered years later, "Donna and I were friends and business partners mostly and it should have probably stayed that way." Even with all those activities and major life changes, Maybelle found the energy to focus once again on baseball.

By the 1970s, the AAGPBL had been largely forgotten, their contribution to baseball and World War II history all but erased. The road back to public recognition for the league was long. Widespread recognition would come with the release of the movie *A League of Their Own* in 1992, but the players' road back to each other began much earlier. For Maybelle Blair, the long road to rediscovery would be life-changing.

In the early 1980s, the former players of the AAGPBL began finding their way back to one another. Former players who had remained friends after the league ended began talking about having a reunion of all former All-Americans. It took years to realize their dream, but eventually the group was successful. Maybelle was aware of their efforts, but it wasn't until she retired from Northrop in 1986, just before the league's first national reunion, that she became fully involved in the efforts to reunite and to tell the world about the history of the AAGPBL.

The origin of that first national reunion began with the league's host families. Throughout the league's existence, players had often lived with local families. These host families, as they were called, were very protective of the players and many stayed connected with the women long after the league ended. Two of those hosts, Arnold Bauer, an usher for the South Bend Blue Sox, his wife, and another host, Ed Des Lauriers, first set out to "find our girls."[2] Des Lauriers and Bauer sent out over 400 letters to former players and got 148 responses.[3] The survey asked about the players' families, about marriage and children, and about whether they had gone back to school or to work. It also inquired about their continued interest in, and participation in, sports. In their responses, former players expressed interest in having a league reunion. At that time, Des Lauriers and Bauer did not follow up on the idea of a reunion, but, unbeknownst to them and fortunately for the league, a few of the players had already been thinking about how to reunite the players.

During a visit with June Peppas, Dorothy "Kammie" Kamenshek and Marge Wenzell were also talking about reuniting players. Over the years since the league ended, all three had been collecting the addresses of players. The combined lists meant they had a very good start on efforts to contact former AAGPBL players. Peppas owned a printing company, so she sent letters to every player, manager, coach, and league personnel she could. In those letters, she asked about the possibility of a reunion and requested information about other players who were not yet found.[4] The response was positive and helpful. In January 1981, Peppas sent out a newsletter that would become the catalyst for the player reunions and the world's reintroduction to the league.

The newsletter consisted of one typed page, but the impact was powerful. In February of the same year, Peppas sent another newsletter because, "Our response last month was fantastic . . . so I decided that another issue was in order." This version of the newsletter went to 130 individuals and was, in the opinion of Peppas, the "first real newsletter."[5] In the second newsletter Peppas requested more information about former players and urged players to report back about their lives after participating in the league. The response to this letter was even greater, and another was sent out in March 1981. Unlike the earlier versions of the newsletter, which were primarily requests for players' contact information, the March version included not only more addresses but also an "In Memory of . . ." section and old photographs of their days in the league. This was the first edition of the newsletter in which Peppas began to call for a national reunion. An edition of the newsletter went out every month after that one. The journey back to each other had begun in earnest.

Maybelle was aware of these attempts to contact former players and the calls for reunions, but, in the early 1980s, she was recovering from a heart condition, still working full-time at Northrop, and still running from Teddy! "I swear to God. I bought houses, moved, had episodes with other women, but she would not leave me alone. About every month Teddy would tell me, 'I'm leaving Swannie. I am done.' She never did. And because she was so darn cute and I was so damn weak, I moved." Despite her "moving all over California," the newsletters and surveys found their way to Maybelle. "I kept an eye on that stuff and of course I was still friends with a lot of the girls. At first, I thought I'm close enough to some of those women," she said with a laugh. "I don't really need a reunion."

It was in the summer of 1981 that Peppas hosted a picnic for former players at her home in Michigan. The event was a success so, in the next newsletter, she reported that plans for more gatherings were already in place. Some former South Bend Blue Sox players also organized a reunion, which took place in August 1981. And then, in September of that year, the Fort Wayne Women's Bureau sponsored an event called, "Run, Jane, Run—Women in Sports." The event was a celebration of women in all sports, but the former baseball players in the area used the event as a reunion of former Fort Wayne Daisies. There was a three-inning exhibition game between the former players and the developmental players known during the league's existence as Junior Daisies. Still employed and recovering from heart surgery, Maybelle was not able to attend any of the 1981 gatherings. "I couldn't go," she said, "but I did keep a curious eye on the events." It seemed clear to Blair that this was the beginning of something bigger, and she did not want to lose track. So, they continued to plan, and Maybelle continued to watch and wait.

Blair was correct, those events were indeed the beginning of bigger things. By September 1981, the newsletters were dedicated to the creation of a national reunion. The first task was to find someone to lead the efforts to organize a large national reunion. Ruth Davis, a South Bend Blue Sox bat girl, volunteered to organize the reunion. "I think . . . perhaps that is the greatest legacy of the League, that it presented a model for all of us growing up at that time that we could do whatever we set our minds to—because we didn't know that we couldn't."[6] Davis's "can do" spirit, along with Peppas's newsletter, made the organization of the reunion possible.

The first national reunion of the AAGPBL was set for July 1982 in Chicago. Because Philip Wrigley, owner of the Chicago Cubs, had created the league, and because many of the former players still lived in the Midwest, Chicago was the logical place. The four-day gathering included a number of events, such as a Chicago Cubs game, a golf outing, and a banquet. But it was the reminiscing, the catching up, that made the trip worth it for many of the former players. After the reunion, June Peppas and Ruth Davis wrote in the next newsletter,

> It was a beautiful experience to be part of the reunion of so many wonderful people. . . . The lobby [of the reunion hotel] became the scene of the world's biggest love-in! If it never happens again, it happened this once—a reunion to be duplicated and always to be remembered in everyone's hearts—Forever.[7]

Despite the fears that this was a once-in-a-lifetime event, reunions continued. The next one was planned for Fort Wayne in 1986, and the one after that was set for 1988 in Scottsdale, Arizona. This would be Maybelle's first. The proximity of the Scottsdale reunion and the fact it was hosted by her old friend Sophie Kurys spurred Blair to attend. "God, we had so much fun in those days. We were all younger then, so we had all kinds of events, outings, golf, and Sophie even had a hayride for us. A lot of the girls were from the city, and I guess they'd never seen hay. Sophie was so proud of that damn hayride." The players were only in their fifties at that point, and most had continued to play sports throughout their lives, so the earlier reunions were very active. That fact and the sheer number of players meant the reunions drew more attention than they do today. Local newspapers and news outlets arrived, wanting to interview the former players and to learn about the league and its role in World War II. As a result, a trickle of information began to appear about this women's baseball league that most people had never heard of before.

In those days, "We were a well-kept secret," Blair remembered. "Most of the country was in the dark about the league. Even if we did try to talk about playing baseball, people would say, 'you mean softball, women don't play baseball.'" That comment was repeated thousands of times to nearly every ballplayer who tried to discuss her experience in the AAGPBL, and eventually they simply stopped trying. Not everyone was surprised to learn about the league, though. In fact, filmmakers Kelly Candaele and Kim Wilson had already begun work on a documentary they called *A League of Their Own*. Candaele was the son of former player Helen Callaghan, and Wilson was a filmmaker. Kelly, who had grown up with stories of the league, wanted to "share a part of my mom's life and to honor her experience and achievements."[8] The documentary was based on interviews, film footage from the National Archives, and many pictures and keepsakes from the players themselves. A Public Broadcast System (PBS) station agreed to pay for a director and to fly a production team to Fort Wayne for the 1986 reunion. There, more players were interviewed, and the filmmakers were able "to capture the special bond that exists between those women." Because she had not attended the earlier reunions, Maybelle was not part of the documentary. But she knew about it and was well aware that the film had become a catalyst for further organization and growth.

While in Fort Wayne, former players, including Karen Kunkel, Dottie Collins, and Fran Janssen, along with supporters Sharon Roepke and Janis Taylor, began talking about creating a formal organization that would help with the long-term goal of recognition and preservation of the former league. To those women, the documentary was exciting, but ultimately they saw it as a first step in gaining the recognition they sought. In May 1987, those women and a handful of others met at the home of Janssen to discuss the establishment of a formal organization and to decide how to best build on the excitement of the newly produced documentary about them. The first step was to create the All-American Girls Professional Baseball League Players Association. In the period between May 23, 1987, and July 20, 1987, the group established the Association as a nonprofit and filed its articles of incorporation with the state of Michigan. Realizing that they would need the help and expertise of younger professionals, such as historians and attorneys, to help them, the group decided to include a membership level for those who had never played baseball; such members were called "Associates." From the beginning, Associates were a huge asset to the organization, and, even today, they are the ones who have kept the group alive. Before the next reunion in 1988, the AAGPBLPA was fully established and ready for work.[9]

As a result of the organization and the force and passion of its leaders, during the Scottsdale reunion, the players agreed to begin a full-on push to gain recognition by the National Baseball Hall of Fame, located in Cooperstown, New York. Pepper Paire reminded the players that, while it was a good thing to be remembered in film, there was a lot left to do. She sang the praises of a film that highlighted them but urged her former teammates not to be complacent. "Pretty fantastic, huh gals?? We will be immortalized on celluloid for the future! . . . Perhaps a film on the AAGPBL might be the trumpet to topple the 'Walls of the Great Baseball Hall of Fame!'"[10] There was intense disagreement among the All-Americans about whether or not they should seek inclusion into the National Baseball Hall of Fame as inductees. Arguing that no one player in the league would qualify, some of the players, including Blair, thought that an exhibit honoring all women in baseball was the best goal. Many of the league members did not want a display; nor did they want to share an exhibit with other women in baseball. Instead, they wanted the entire league to be inducted into the Hall as a single honorary member, which would include a ceremony and full recognition. While most of the players knew and understood that many women played, coached, and umpired baseball outside their league, they argued that theirs was the first professional women's league and should therefore have a special place in the Hall of Fame.

Recognition by the National Baseball Hall of Fame became a priority of those leading the charge so, after a great deal of negotiation (and stubbornness), their efforts paid off. Ted Spencer, the Hall of Fame's curator, began communicating with representatives of the league. Shortly after that he entered into negotiations to get the AAGPBL players recognized by the Hall. Spencer assured the group that the Hall's leadership wanted to do an exhibit, but that space and a lack of memorabilia were concerns.[11] Once assured that there would be no problem with finding items to display and with the full support of Spencer, serious negotiations between the National Baseball Hall of Fame and the AAGPBL began.

Spencer successfully negotiated a compromise. There would be a "Women in Baseball" exhibit, and the Hall would have an unveiling ceremony to honor the women. After a great deal of discussion and disagreement, the membership agreed to this proposal, and the date was set for the league's recognition by the National Baseball Hall of Fame.[12] Blair remembered the discussions about this "compromise" with a laugh. "I was never for us being 'inducted,' you know, an actual induction. Some of the girls thought we were better than we were. We don't belong there like the men do. But I do like that women are recognized at the Hall of Fame. That is a big deal, and we celebrated it." One hundred and fifty former players from the AAGPBL, along with countless friends and family members, met in Cooperstown on November 3, 1988, for the three-day event. A former player and the person who kept the dream of Hall of Fame recognition alive, Dottie Collins, along with Hall of Fame president Howard Talbot, pulled the cord to unveil the "Women in Baseball" exhibit. As Ted Spencer remembered years later,

> Here's a day where we [normally] have four hundred people. That's what we'd have on a Saturday in November, 400 people. [But] the place was packed, and they sang that [AAGPBL] song all day long. . . . And this museum had never had that much noise! It was great. . . . To me it changed the whole direction of the museum because it brought home how important the game is culturally.[13]

The event at the Hall of Fame was everything the former players could have hoped for, and most of them were happy to rest, knowing they were finally getting some recognition. Little did they know that their time in the spotlight was just beginning.

Figure 1 Maybelle Blair, circa 1930 (author's collection).

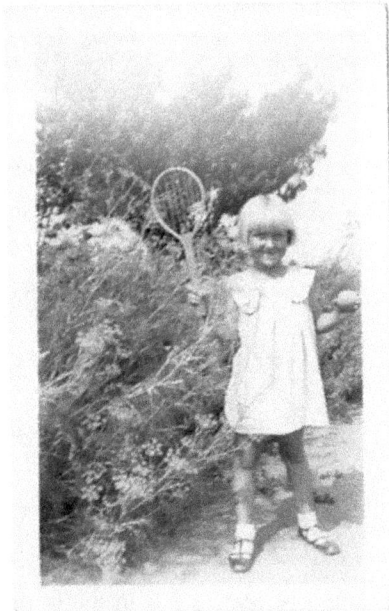

Figure 2 New tennis racquet, circa 1933 (author's collection).

Figure 3 Bud in front of the family house (author's collection).

Figure 4 The Chicago Cardinals. Maybelle is in the center, fourth from the left (author's collection).

Figure 5 Maybelle at a stop on her way to South Dakota, 1966 (author's collection).

Figure 6 Jenai pictured at same stop en route to South Dakota, 1966 (author's collection).

Figure 7 From left to right, Maybelle, Rod, and Peggy, 1966 (author's collection).

Figure 8 Rod Blair during a visit from Blair and Jenai, 1966 (author's collection).

Figure 9 Maybelle, George, and Peggy, 1966 (author's collection).

Figure 10 One of the aircraft Blair guided through the streets of Los Angeles (author's collection).

Figure 11 Penny Marshall at the tryouts for *A League of Their Own* (author's collection).

Figure 12 Maybelle and Shirley Burkovich at Beyer Stadium, 2015 (author's collection).

Figure 13 Jane Moffet and Maybelle at the 2010 reunion in Detroit (author's collection).

Figure 14 Maybelle at first Baseball For All National Tournament, 2015 (author's collection).

Figure 15 Shirley Burkovich coaching at the first Baseball For All National Tournament, 2015 (author's collection).

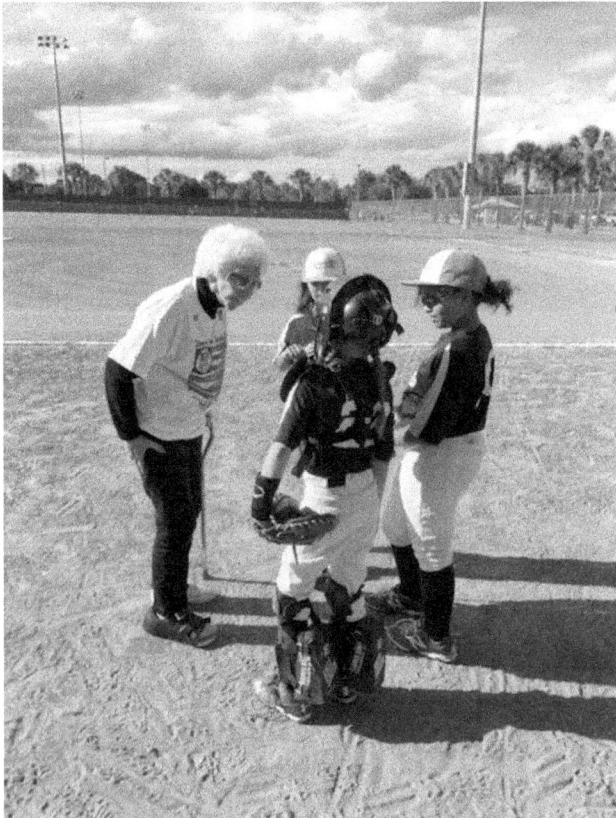

Figure 16 Maybelle coaching at the First Baseball For All National Tournament, 2015 (author's collection).

Figure 17 Maybelle and Shirley meeting a young fan at the 2018 Women's Baseball World Cup, 2018 (author's collection).

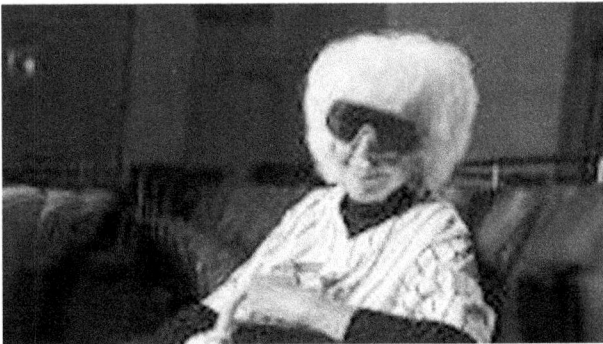

Figure 18 Maybelle at the Coronado Theater in Rockford, Illinois, at the Premiere of the Amazon series *A League of Their Own* (author's collection).

6

UNFORGOTTEN

One of the attendees at the Hall of Fame event in 1988, "Hidden in plain sight behind sunglasses and a baseball cap," was popular Hollywood director, Penny Marshall. "One day I saw a documentary on the All-American Girls Professional Baseball League of the 1940s. It was about a group of courageous women who were recruited to play baseball when the young men had gone off to fight World War II," she recalled.[1] "I thought it was a story that needed to be told, and told with accuracy, inspiration and humor."[2] Soon she secured the rights to the story and to the use of Kelly Candaele's and Kim Wilson's title *A League of Their Own*. Hearing about the Hall of Fame recognition, Marshall jumped at the opportunity to meet the players. She attended the weekend's events, met former players, and left with renewed determination to make a movie about these women, one that would not just tell their story but that would tell it with the appreciation and reverence they deserved. Marshall was more successful than she could have ever dreamed.

Penny Marshall's respect for the players is evident in her decision to include them in making the film. Some worked as advisors on the film, doing everything from offering advice about period dress to coaching Hollywood stars on how to throw a baseball. Karen Kunkel, former player for the Grand Rapid Chicks and a founder of the AAGPBL Players Association, was approached by Marshall and asked to be an advisor for the movie. Kunkel's husband Jack remembered, "One night I pick [the phone] up, and the voice on the other end of the line says, this is Penny Marshall and I wanna talk to Karen Kunkel. Karen talks to her for about a half hour, she hangs up the phone and says, how'd you like to get into the movie business, and I say, what're you talking about So, there was the beginning of *A League of Their Own*."[3]

Penny wanted Karen not only for her experience in playing but also because of her connection with many former players through the Players Association she had created. Karen's role would be as a technical advisor for the film, helping to make the actors look like athletes, which wasn't always easy. Kunkel said in an interview about the film, "Madonna for example could hardly throw so, every day they were working with her arm, working on catching they turned her into quite an athlete."[4] Aside from helping the actors, Karen also acted as a mediator between the AAGPBL and the filmmakers. She set up meetings and even scheduled a large tryout for any former players who were interested. To add authenticity, Marshall hoped there might be a few players with both playing skills and some acting ability. The plan was to use the players themselves as the older players who return to Cooperstown at the end of the movie. The tryouts were scheduled for a small town near Springfield, Illinois.

Certain she was going to be a movie star, Maybelle showed up with her glove in hand and ready to "be a star. You know me, I always thought I could do anything." Like so many of the players, she was great at playing ball, "but couldn't act worth a damn." Marshall picked a few players out of the group and sent them to Wrigley Field, where they had additional auditions. "Well that went south in a hurry." Blair said, "None of 'em could act worth a lick." Maybelle didn't get a speaking role in the movie, but she would get another chance to be included.

Karen Kunkel sent out another letter to the players, inviting anyone interested to come to Cooperstown to be extras in the movie's last scenes. Around fifty women, including Blair, showed up, and for seven days they played games on Doubleday Field and filmed the scenes inside the Hall of Fame. "That was harder work than you'd think. We would do a scene and then laugh and clap for ourselves, then here'd come Penny, 'Do it again.' We'd do the same damn thing one hundred times." The former players gathered on Doubleday Field during the day to rehearse and play softball then hung out at the local pubs in the evening. One result of that week was what Blair called "a reconnection between friends." Another was one of the most memorable sports scenes ever filmed. As some of the players argued over the umpire's call and others lumbered around the bases, "acting like they were twenty again," an audience watches as the haunting lyrics of Madonna's song, "This Used to Be My Playground," sets a nostalgic tone. Blair's hand slapping a ball into her glove is all of her that made the final cut of the film, but she admits even today, "I think what we did in the last few minutes of that movie brought us a lot of attention because it made thousands of women sad for what they didn't get to do and mad because they still can't."

Even being part of the film did not prepare the former players for the impact their movie would have on them and on generations of girls and women in sports. On July 4, 1992, *A League of Their Own* opened and opened the eyes of the world to the women of the AAGPBL and their story. The movie, now a cultural phenomenon, is shown almost daily on one streaming site or another, and young girls recite lines from the movie as if it were current. Finally, after nearly forty years, women's professional baseball reentered the American consciousness. And the lives of former players were changed forever.

The players are very aware that, without the movie, their time as professional baseball players would likely have gone unnoticed. Terry Donahue, Blair's catcher, argues that, if not for the movie, "we would have all been dead and gone and no one would have ever known about us." Of course, as Maybelle Blair has pointed out, the film could never have happened unless the women themselves had started the process. "Nobody [knew about the AAGPBL], nobody did until after the movie. The movie was the making of everybody and even when you mention[ed] that you played in the all American or the National league they [didn't] know what you [were] talking about and could care less, now they care, it's amazing. We wouldn't have the movie, though, if we hadn't had those reunions. That really got us going."[5]

In telling the story of the AAGPBL, the film also changed the lives of the league's players. For many, it opened doors to travel, writing, and, of course, public speaking. To some of the players, the idea that they might write a book, speak in public, or be interviewed for television or radio had seemed far-fetched. After the release of the movie, however, that is exactly what they did. The players travel all over the country, speaking and signing autographs, and have been interviewed countless times on television and radio programs, including CBS's *Sunday Morning*. Terry Donahue remembered how overwhelming it was for them.

> When that [the movie] came out, and the people at work couldn't believe it, that I had played professional. So, it was pretty exciting, oh goodness gracious. You know we were being interviewed, we weren't talkers, and we would never, it was incredible. . . . I said, "Well if you want an interview, come to my apartment," because we were running around like crazy, we all were. We were overwhelmed, really. We couldn't believe that we were getting all of this attention. Because

anytime you mention that movie people go crazy. I think we were really overwhelmed and so excited.[6]

Not only was the league introduced to the world through the movie, but many of the players were also introduced to each other. After attending the Scottsdale reunion, Maybelle never missed another one. Even though they had met briefly in Cooperstown while working on the movie, it was the 1993 South Bend reunion where Maybelle really connected with the woman who would become her dearest friend, Shirley Burkovich. "We had met in Cooperstown but didn't really become friends. She was so quiet. Well, except that damn line in the movie." Most of the players did not have speaking parts in the movie, but those who did continued to get royalty checks. Burkovich proudly cashed a check for $1.97 every month for her line, "Dottie, having you here is good luck."[7] Until Shirley's death in 2022 she and Maybelle argued over who could deliver the line the best. Blair, incensed that she didn't get the line and despite never once saying it correctly, insisted that she would have done a better job.

Shirley Burkovich, a native of Pittsburgh, joined the AAGPBL in 1948 after her brother saw an ad for tryouts. Like so many girls of her generation, Burkovich began playing baseball with her brothers and other boys in her neighborhood. But World War II and the AAGPBL provided something she never thought possible, a chance to play baseball profession-ally. In 1948, with the blessing of her father and the encouragement of her brother, Shirley tried out for the AAGPBL, and, just a few weeks later, she received a letter asking her to report for spring training in Missouri.

Burkovich was only sixteen, and her mother refused to let her report for training alone. So, they both headed to spring training. Once her mother was convinced of the league's legitimacy, she left her daughter and returned to Swissvale, Pennsylvania. Shirley never looked back. She played for the Muskegon Lassies in her first season, then the Chicago Colleens, Springfield Sallies, and, finally, the Rockford Peaches in 1951.

As many of the former players did once the league ended, Shirley found employment. She took a job with Pacific Bell, where she worked until her retirement. "I had to decide between that opportunity to take that job or go back for maybe another one season or maybe two," Burkovich said. "I didn't know how long it was going to last, and so I thought, well, I think I better set myself up for a job that I had a little security." Although she did not play much baseball during the years she worked at the telephone company and did not have a lot of contact with her former teammates, when the AAGPBL players began their road back to one another, Shirley was excited and ready to rejoin the team.

Maybelle and Shirley had very little in common except baseball. Blair is flashy, outgoing, and confident, while Burkovich was quiet, shy, and unsure. Yet, when they met at the baggage claim in the Chicago airport and Shirley asked Blair if she needed a ride to South Bend, a thirty-year friendship and partnership began. Maybelle said of Shirley, "The whole reunion, she didn't say a word just stood back. I guess she didn't know anyone. It bugged me. So, I volunteered her." At the annual meeting held every year at the reunions Blair announced that the girls in California would have the 1995 reunion. Surprised by the unexpected announcement, the AAGPBL board asked Maybelle who was going to help her, and she said, "Shirley Burkovich and Snookie, Lou [Farella], Kammie, [Dottie Kamenshek], and Tiby." None of them, including Shirley, had been consulted ahead of time, and, as Blair remembered, "Shirley nearly died on the spot. I've been volunteering her time ever since."

The 1995 reunion, held in Indian Wells, California, was a big hit. Looking back on that reunion, the first of many that Blair helped to host, she said, "that was probably the best reunion we ever had. I think it set the standard for all the others." In 1995, many of the former players were in their 50s and 60s, and most were still in good physical shape. "Because a lot of the girls were still active then, we had competitions." Blair remembered the fun of what they called the Olympics. "That reunion was the first time we had the Olympics. There were events like the baseball throw, Ping-Pong, swimming among other events. I swear you'd have thought it was the real Olympics. You know how competitive ballplayers are, even when they can't play anymore. They nearly killed themselves running after the damn Ping-Pong ball." For three days, the former players competed against each other, toured local California sights, and had the times of their lives.

In addition to competitions and sightseeing, the reunion also featured a *League of Their Own*–themed "suds bucket" night and a "western dance" night. Ann Meyers was the keynote speaker for the banquet. Meyers, a former basketball player, was the first woman to sign an NBA contract. She signed with the Indiana Pacers in 1979 and later became a WNBA team owner. "Most of the girls hadn't met too many famous women athletes," Blair said. "Most knew who she was, though, and Annie was great. She really seemed to enjoy being with us." Blair and Shirley worked closely on the planning for the reunion, and, later, Shirley would admit that, while the experience was scary, she was proud of the work they did.

The 1995 reunion of the AAGPBL Players Association may have set the standard for future reunions, but it also solidified the friendship between Maybelle and Shirley. After the reunion, the group of Californians continued to meet for lunch and attend local baseball and softball events. Despite her shyness, Shirley was swept along with the group as they rekindled their friendships. Over the years, she continued to be friends with the other women in the group, but it was her tie to Maybelle that changed both their lives and the lives of future generations of girls. Shirley and Maybelle were both retired by the time they met, and both had a deep-seated commitment to women's sports. They believed that the world needed to know the history of girls and women in the game and that every girl should have the same opportunity they did to play baseball. The AAGPBL Players Association was barely ten years old when the two began a partnership that Blair said, "lasted longer than most marriages." As it is with most nonprofits, the quest for money to operate the organization was constant. Fortunately for the association, Maybelle had a knack for making money. Blair used her business sense, dedication, and boundless energy to raise funds for the Players Association. "One of the first things you have to do," she explained, "is to let people know you exist and then to convince them that you matter. That's what me and Shirley did for years." Maybelle may have been the early catalyst, but she readily admits that she and Shirley were a team. At first Shirley was reluctant to be out front and visible. Later, though, she accepted and even relished her role as part of the duo.

In what was quite possibly the epitome of an odd couple, Maybelle and Shirley teamed up to host four reunions, including a reunion on a cruise in 2008. Maybelle kept bringing up the idea of a cruise, but the members of the AAGPBL Players Association board kept resisting the idea, saying, "The players can't afford a cruise," "How would we have our banquet or meeting?" and "No one will go." Maybelle remembered, "They said we couldn't do it, but I was stubborn. Shirly was even determined that we could do it. She wouldn't have said it to them, but when they told us, 'You all will never pull that off' she said, 'watch us.'" For a year and a half, Maybelle, Shirley, and Jane Moffet, former player and past vice president of the Players Association, worked to design and then produce a calendar that included every All-American who had a baseball card. It was a huge hit, and that, as well as other fundraisers, produced enough money for every former ballplayer to attend the reunion free of charge. "It was all paid for with that calendar. I had the idea, but Jane Moffet put it together. That thing made money hand over fist. We paid for everybody's cruise. Everybody's. Associates, players, everybody. And we made money for the association," Maybelle recalled. Many of the players had never been on a cruise, so they jumped at the opportunity. The association met at a hotel in Fort Lauderdale a day before they were to set sail so they could have their annual business meeting. The next morning, the All-Americans set sail for a five-day cruise.

There were, of course, hundreds of other passengers on the ship, most of whom had only a passing curiosity about the women as they walked around the ship in their AAGPBL hats and shirts. Like most cruise ships, this one was large and had a magnificent central stairway that rose the full three stories of the ship. One evening, as the players waited to enter the dining room, they gathered on the stairs and, with no prompting, began singing the league song. Their voices filled the central portion of the ship, and on all three stories people stopped what they were doing to listen. When the song ended, there was silence for what seemed like several seconds as people tried to take in what they had just witnessed. Then there was an explosion of applause and then, as was often the case, the women were engulfed by fans and well-wishers. They pulled off that cruise reunion, spread the word about the AAGPBL and their role in history to a new audience, and helped to give some of the players an experience they would never have had.

The partnership of Maybelle and Shirley brought more than exciting reunions to the players. Their exploits fueled much of the growth of the Players Association and quite literally raised money to keep the association afloat. "We started designing T-shirts and had them made, and off we went. Every Saturday and Sunday we were busy during baseball season selling T-shirts and things at Little League games, semi pro games, ladies slow-pitch softball. We went from San Francisco clear down to San Diego and doing that. If there was a game, we were there, and there were a lot of games going, a lot of tournaments." Because of the movie, the players' own attempts to spread their stories, and a growing following among female athletes, Maybelle and Shirley helped to change the landscape of women's baseball.

The experiences also changed both of them—especially Shirley. "We were up and down the interstate, Shirl and me. Anytime someone called and said, 'Hey we are having a tournament,' we'd go and sell our stuff for the All-Americans. We threw out more first pitches than Nolan Ryan, watched more Little League games than we could count, and signed more baseballs than I ever knew existed," Blair remembered with a laugh. "And during most of that time Shirley never said a word. I kept telling her to speak up, to say something." Publicly it seemed like Shirley was too meek to stand up to Blair, too shy to defend herself, or even weak. But, as Maybelle recalled, nothing could have been further from the truth. "Unfortunately, she listened and started fussing at ME! No one else, just me. She'd say 'Maybelle, you can't do that. It's against the rules.' Or 'Maybelle, you can't say that.' I swear to God, I coulda killed her sometimes." Their public presence, that of the flashy, outgoing Maybelle and the shy, accommodating Shirley, was endearing, giving the pair an opportunity to touch the lives of even more would-be baseball players. In an interview a few years before she died, Shirley said of her and Blair's partnership, "I think there are a lot of girls out there like me, quiet and shy. It's good for them to see me too. Maybelle is always talking, and people see her. Some girls don't relate to that, though."[8] The friendship, the partnership, their banter, and the ways in which both women served individually and jointly as role models changed the lives of girls and women around the world. It also gave Shirley an opportunity to grow and change. "I really did start to speak some, I guess," Shirley said. With her voice and her heart, Shirley Burkovich spoke volumes.

The movie *A League of Their Own* may have been the world's first introduction to the AAGPBL, but, when players like Maybelle and Shirley ventured out to meet girls and women who played baseball and softball, they realized that they had a unique opportunity to really make a difference in the lives of girls by opening up about their sporting experiences. They talked about women's sports, taught the virtues of sport, and urged girls to demand more. Their impact was great.

> We [Shirley and Maybelle] started working with other ex-major-league ball players on free clinics for girls and boys. The clinics used to be strictly for the boys, and then we started going out and saying in these clinics—girls and boys and there was a group of us, some ex-Dodgers and ex-Angels that they put together this group called Sports Educators of America—and we went out, this was just in the Southern California area, and we would go out and do these free baseball clinics for the kids and we would try to incorporate education and sports. Telling the kids that education is just as important because you ask the kids, who wants to be a major-league ball player? Well, everybody raises their hand, so then you say to them, well, all right, there are seven hundred positions in major-league baseball, what if you don't make it, then what? So, we tell them that they've got to have something to fall back on, so we start stressing education in sports to these kids, trying to encourage them to stay in school and have a backup just in case they don't make it in the baseball world. I can always relate to that because that's what happened

to me. I thought baseball was always going to be my career, and I didn't plan for anything else. Fortunately, I [Shirley] got a job at the telephone company, and at that time the companies were more like families. The telephone company was like a family, so I had the opportunity to work for them, so that's what we have been doing now for the last ten or fifteen years, going out to these clinics and working with young people.[9]

Sports should not be just for boys, they argued. "Everyone, even girls, should have a chance to play because if they do, their lives will be changed forever." For years, Blair and Shirley traveled to bring that message to anyone who would listen. "It's like that runway thing you were talking about," she told me. "Shirl and I went up and down the California coast from one baseball diamond to another digging runways. I mean we didn't think about it like that then. But we were sure determined." As she had done since those early days on that dusty homemade field across from her family home, Maybelle continued creating baseball opportunities well into retirement.

For Maybelle, traveling to raise money and spread the word about women's baseball was simply not enough. Signing autographs or throwing out first pitches brought them and the league some fame, but Maybelle started talking about more. She began to talk about how there needs to be a place for women's baseball to be honored and celebrated and a place where girls can come to learn the game—another "League of Their Own." "We need to have a place where our papers and documents are kept. A place where our old photographs and uniforms are kept and preserved." But, as her grandiose ideas often were, this one was deemed impossible, too much. The Players Association board decided that having such a place was unnecessary. Shirley had been appointed to fill a vacant seat on the board in 2000. Always the rule follower, when the board discouraged the idea and declared the History Museum in South Bend, Indiana, as the official repository of AAGPBL papers, Shirley acquiesced. Maybelle never thought the History Museum in South Bend was the right place for their artifacts and papers to be held. Thinking it was too scattered in its focus and without any connection to baseball, she argued for the creation of a separate museum that would be dedicated only to women's baseball. This put the two women on opposite sides of an issue that was important to Blair, and, as she remembered, it caused a rift between them.

"Shirley made me so mad. She saw the same things I did but that damn board had her convinced she had to follow along. We still traveled around together, and we were still friends, but I was mad, and she knew it." Tired of the fight, one day Shirley said to Blair, "well if you don't like the way the board is doing things, why don't you run for a seat?" She did. Maybelle was elected to the board in 2011. "I think Shirley thought that if I was on the board I would follow the rules and just be satisfied with the way things were. I wasn't." Being on the board of directors did not alter Blair's quest for change; nor did it dampen her resolve. It simply gave her another platform from which to make those pleas to the association.

The friction between Shirley and Maybelle intensified, then eased, in a never-ending cycle. When Maybelle had a new idea and got vocal about it, Shirley felt uneasy and torn between her friend and her loyalty to the association and to the board. Blair got mad at Shirley for not speaking up. Then another invitation to represent the league and raise funds would emerge and off they'd go together, a team. On and on it went. Undeterred by Shirley, or the board and its rules, Maybelle kept talking about creating a museum for women's baseball. Eventually she solicited the help of former players Karen Kunkel and Jane Moffet and a handful of like-minded associate members, and a full-on push for a museum, a place of their own, was on. This time, uneasy about it, but intrigued, Shirley asked, "Why not?"

The crack in Shirley's resolve was smaller than her dedication to the board or her innate need to follow the rules, but it was there. This fact gave Maybelle some hope and her fellow board members a pause. "We started talking about having a place of our own, a museum. And the board kept saying no, no, no, can't do that. We ignored them and kept talking about it, so they started sending out surveys to all the former players to show us they were right." With questions such as, "Do you have memorabilia? How much? What do you want to do with it? Do you want a museum?" The board set out to prove that a museum wasn't possible or wanted. The results were always mixed, and usually it was easy to tell who filled out a survey by how the person responded to the questions. Still, they continued to send the surveys. And it became clear to Blair that the only real reason to send them was that it delayed any further discussion of a separate museum or archives. Even mild-mannered Shirley got frustrated.

In the beginning, Maybelle, Shirley, Jane, and Karen thought the best plan was to purchase a building in Cooperstown, along Main Street and down from the National Baseball Hall of Fame. Thinking that baseball-loving fans would also be interested in their museum, Cooperstown seemed like a logical setting. The group even contacted a real-estate agent and priced a building in Cooperstown. The board members were so upset that they set up a meeting for the next reunion so that the two sides could present their proposals to the organization. The meeting was contentious from the beginning and only resulted in a split between the board of directors and a very determined Maybelle and Shirley.

That meeting did nothing to solve the issue of a museum, but it did mark a shift in Shirley. She got tired of being told no by the board but continued to respect the fact that people had different views. Eventually the rift within the organization took a malicious turn. Shirley was a fair, kind-hearted person, and loyal. When the attacks by the board became personal and primarily focused on Maybelle and a few others, Shirley had enough. In 2013, after thirteen years in service to the AAGPBLPA, Shirley resigned from the board. Maybelle followed, as did two other board members. Those resignations caused a split in the Players Association that continues.

Leaving the Players Association board of directors was a very difficult decision for Shirley, but neither she nor Maybelle was deterred from pursuing their dream of a museum or from supporting girls and women in sports. They continued to represent the AAGPBL and women's baseball at events around the country. "We did those RBI clinics at Angel Stadium and Dodger Stadium. At first Tiby and Snookie went with Shirley and me then they stopped, and Shirley and I kept going. Because we kept going, we met more people and got more involved in things. Girl's baseball things." Connections that proved to be significant later began in those clinics.

During baseball clinics at Dodger Stadium, Maybelle and Shirley met people who would become influential in their lives and important to women in baseball. Kim Ng was the assistant general manager for the Dodgers between 2002 and 2011. Blair and Shirley became friends with Ng, and, significantly, Kim became a vocal supporter of the pair and their dream. In 2021, Kim became the first woman to be hired as a major-league general manager. Maybelle was one of the first people Ng called when she got the job.

Blair and Shirley also connected with one of the most significant women in the growth of girl's baseball, Baseball For All (BFA) founder Justine Siegal. The group started with one all-girls team playing in Cooperstown, New York, at a tournament. Now they have players in forty states and five countries playing baseball in leagues and in tournaments.[10] Maybelle and Shirley met Justine soon after BFA was founded, and, as Blair recalled, "we supported what Justine was doing right away. We could tell she was going to be successful. And we just loved those girls." Their connection to BFA was important for everyone involved. The partnership boosted the visibility of BFA and put a whole new spin on the museum project. The museum project that Maybelle and Shirley first envisioned was about preserving the history of girls and women in the game. Now, it would also include a place for girls to make history of their own—on a field of their own.

The connection to Kim Ng and to Justine Siegal was important to Maybelle and Shirley personally, but their influence and guidance also inspired the pair to do more on behalf of girls and women in baseball. Blair and Shirley continued to travel around to tournaments, clinics, and events, highlighting women in the game. They soon became the most recognizable faces in the fight to include girls in baseball. With every appearance they won over new fans and convinced more people that women did deserve a place of their own.

In June 2015, BFA held its first national thirteen-and-under tournament in Orlando, Florida. Maybelle and Shirley, now aged eighty-eight and eighty-two, were there signing autographs and cheering as 150 girls took the field in their own tournament. At the closing ceremonies Maybelle and Shirley were asked to lead the crowd in singing the All-American's song. They began to sing and then stood watching in awe as a crowd of young girls, from eight to thirteen years of age, and their parents sang to them. "Wow, they knew the song, all of it, every word," Shirley said, shaking her head.[11] From that day until Shirley's death, the pair never missed a BFA National tournament. Maybelle went alone to the last one, which was difficult for her. "Shirl would want me to continue, so I am. I miss her, but we still have work to do. So, I gotta keep going."

Maybelle's lifelong quest to create baseball opportunities for girls and women certainly did not end when she retired, because, as she said, "I can never retire from baseball. You can't just retire from something that's in your blood." Even the death of Shirley in 2022 did not stop her progress. The methods, the path, and even the allies changed over time, but the goals did not. Whether it was selling AAGPBL merchandise at softball tournaments, attending clinics, doing interviews, planning reunions, or serving on the AAGPBL board, Maybelle's mission continued. At times that goal morphed, grew, seemed reachable then unattainable, but nothing dampened her resolve. When obstacles emerged, she simply figured out a way around them.

7

THE INTERNATIONAL WOMEN'S BASEBALL CENTER

The next decade of Maybelle Blair's life was dedicated to a new organization, one that would help sustain her dream and determination to create a home for women's baseball and a solid foundation for the development of another league of their own, another baseball league just for women. Even when she lost the backing of the AAGPBL, Maybelle never stopped dreaming or scheming about ways to build a home of their own. As she had done at every stage of her life, when thrown a curve, she "simply stepped out of the batter's box and refocused." This time, the result was the creation of the International Women's Baseball Center (IWBC).

By 2013, Maybelle had resigned from the AAGPBL Players Association. She continued to represent the league and attend reunions and never slowed down her support of putting girls on the field. Blair realized that the AAGPBL was never going to embrace her and Shirley Burkovich's dream of a museum or even accept it as legitimate. "I decided pretty quick that we didn't need the All-Americans, but Shirley kept thinking they would come around. So, we tried to work with them. Even after we all resigned from the board we tried." A lack of support neither surprised nor deterred Maybelle, but when a difference of opinion turned into personal and professional attacks, she and Shirley had enough. Together with Karen Kunkel, Jane Moffet, Donna Cohen, and me (Kat D. Williams), they created a new organization. The IWBC was founded on February 22, 2014, in Blair's living room in Sunset Beach, California.

Despite the negativity she experienced, Maybelle benefited from her time on the board of the AAGPBL. From traveling to softball tournaments to public appearances at Major League Baseball's Fanfest to countless interviews, Maybelle made a name for herself that she was able to use to help get the IWBC off the ground. Women's baseball was popular around the world and gaining popularity in the United States in 2014, with a number of organizations dedicated to helping build the sport for girls. The time was right, Maybelle and Shirley were ready, and with confidence and determination they used the threads of friendship, teamwork, and baseball to create a group dedicated to preserving the long and expansive history of women's baseball.

The women who came together in Blair's living room all agreed that the preservation of their stories was important, but they also understood how important it was to use that history as a way to empower future generations of girls. Armed with the knowledge of the past and the desire to create a future for girls in baseball, the group gathered over pizza and beer to discuss what seemed to them to be a glaring absence in the world of sports: a home for women's baseball. Maybelle, sitting in "her chair," a cracked and worn formerly white rocker, directed the conversation as those who were not former AAGPBL players scrambled to take notes. There should be a Hall of Fame, one woman said, and a museum, said another. With what sounded like twenty voices speaking all at once, the women called out their desires for the new home of women's baseball. "Oh, there should be an educational center, and a place where girls and women can go to play, learn to coach, and umpire." And when Shirley quietly said, "it should also be a place where everyone can learn about and enjoy the game," the entire room loudly agreed. Out of that meeting came the IWBC and a determination to challenge the myth that girls and women don't play baseball.

The group of women, most of whom had no experience at doing so, created what would become an internationally recognized nonprofit organization. From our vantage point, sitting in Maybelle's living room, all of those dreams seemed possible. On yellow legal pads, we wrote names, ideas, goals, and, admittedly, some unrealistic expectations: "Let's contact Billie Jean King. She'll help." "What about Hillary Clinton or Michelle Obama?" "Let's reach out to Major League Baseball, they'll help." In hindsight, the naivete is obvious, but the dedication to the cause of women's baseball was real and only increased as the IWBC solidified and grew. Putting the goals, the dreams, and the grandiose claims on paper made what had previously been a wild dream seem possible.

One of the first steps was to write a mission statement, which was also done that day. It read,

> At the IWBC, education is the cornerstone of our mission to protect, preserve, and promote all aspects of women's baseball, both on and off the field. We strive to inspire the next generation of players by helping

them realize their dreams not only of participating in the sport, but also of passing on all they will learn and achieve for generations to come.

Within days, one of the founders, and the group's attorney, Donna Cohen, was tasked with the process of making the IWBC an official non-profit and of introducing the group to a growing collection of women's baseball advocates. Cohen recently recalled that "they shipped me out to make friends and connections in the women's baseball world. What a fabulous adventure."[1] Donna's efforts brought the organization into the growing conversation about women's baseball, resulting in the IWBC gaining official nonprofit status and a place at what Maybelle called "the baseball table." Despite the fact that many involved in the IWBC were fans of and knowledgeable about women's baseball, there was no central place for the group to go for information, no place where they could meet others with similar interests and goals. Out of need, the creation of that central place, a repository of information and contacts, also became a goal of the IWBC.

For the first year, the IWBC worked to carve out a place for itself. IWBC members attended girls' tournaments, met important figures in the game, and solidified relationships within baseball. From the very beginning, IWBC members knew that the IWBC needed to fill several voids in the world of women's baseball: education, preservation, and participation were at the top of the list. We set out to fill those voids. Fortunately, naivete and good luck were our allies in those early days.

In addition to tracking down people thought to be important in the world of women's baseball and showing up to as many events as possible, IWBC members sought other ways to introduce the IWBC to the world. Each of us had contacts with whom to share and opportunities in which to tell our story, and each of us reached out to our contacts and took our opportunities. As a native Louisvillian, I visit the city often, and, on one visit, a Saturday afternoon in the spring of 2014, I walked into the Louisville Slugger Museum & Factory and asked to speak to someone in charge of creating events. An assistant to P. J. Shelley, director of education and programing, emerged. While she was not the person in charge, she was a fan of women's baseball, and, thankfully, as it turned out, so was Shelley. It did not take much convincing for the museum to agree to host the first ever Women's Baseball Symposium in the summer of 2014.

With no more than twenty participants in the audience, the IWBC launched itself from a stage provided by the Louisville Slugger Museum & Factory. Maybelle Blair, Shirley Burkovich, and I spoke about the importance of preserving the history of women's baseball and of using that history to encourage and empower the current generation of girls who play the game. The audience was small, but, on that weekend, we made contacts that still help to sustain us. The next year, the museum hosted the IWBC for a second symposium. This time, additional AAGPBL players and other women involved in women's baseball participated, and the crowd was larger. After the panels, an autograph session gave the public an opportunity to meet the former players. "This is how we do it," Blair said. "Show people we are here, and just want to play and be part of the game. Don't ask 'em. Tell 'em." Bolstered by the success of the symposium and the confidence and dedication of Shirley and Maybelle, the group set out to do just that.

The Blair and Burkovich team traveled up and down the West Coast, raising awareness about the IWBC and the need for a physical location, a home, for girls and women in baseball. No one, including Maybelle and Shirley, was prepared for the overwhelming lack of excitement about the idea. Unlike those from the AAGPBL who opposed the idea, the public was not hostile to them or the concept. They simply ignored it. It seemed much of the baseball–loving public still believed that boys play baseball and girls play softball or that the only time and place that women played was in the 1940s when the AAGPBL was at its peak. The very basic idea that girls and women have always been part of the game and that they should be able to be now was a new idea to a lot of people. Convincing them otherwise was a difficult task, but one that had to be successfully completed before we could sell the public on the importance of a place of their own! Still, Maybelle, determined as ever, and Shirley continued to show up at tournaments and even represented the AAGPBL at national baseball events, where they talked about the need for a place of their own. They were unable to get traction for the museum idea until the place for a place of their own revealed itself to them.

By 2015, umpire and women's baseball advocate Perry Barber had joined the board of the IWBC. She frequently traveled around the country, umpiring tournaments, and one of her annual stops was in Rockford, Illinois, for the all-women's Peach Orchard Classic Baseball Tournament. Rockford is well known for its AAGPBL team, the Rockford Peaches. The baseball tournament was held at Beyer Stadium, where the Peaches played from 1943 to 1954. Standing near her car in the parking lot, Perry overhead a conversation between her colleague, Drew Hoffman, and Greg Schwanke of the Friends of Beyer Stadium. "You know anyone involved in women's baseball who might want some buildings or some property?" She heard Greg ask Drew. Sitting across the street from Beyer Stadium, former home of the renowned Rockford Peaches, sat two dilapidated buildings on unused property. Perry overheard the conversation, and later that night she called me to relay the exchange. The answer was of course, "Yes. Yes, we do."

Within two months, Maybelle joined Shirley, Donna, and me as we visited Rockford. The Winnebago County chairman and other representatives of the city welcomed us and vowed to help get the property donated to the group and provide the money to raze the buildings and clean up the site. The place, our place, was Rockford. Of course it was Rockford—the home of the best-known women's baseball team in history and a city known historically as "the cradle of baseball."

Rockford has a storied history in sports and, especially, in baseball. In part this is because of local Rockford players, such as Albert Spalding, eventual founder of the Spalding & Bros. Corporation, a world-renowned sporting-goods company, and Ross Barnes, one of the most influential players of the mid-nineteenth century. In 1896, Rockford became what the *New York Times* called the "the cradle of the great American sport in the West."[2] During and immediately after the Civil War, baseball was growing in popularity and quickly caught the attention of both men. Spalding and Barnes both played with the local baseball clubs, the Rockford Pioneers and the Forest City's. The men were part of the Forest City's team that gained national attention when Rockford upset the "seemingly invincible National Club of Washington," which had embarked on one of the first tours in baseball history. The Forest City's subsequently enjoyed "phenomenal success" and also toured nationally.[3] Spalding and Barnes were eventually recruited by the Boston Red Stockings and later went on to play for the Chicago White Stockings.[4] By the late nineteenth century, both men had retired as players, but, following his retirement, Spalding went on to promote and advance baseball through his sporting-goods company and his "official" *Baseball Guides*.

Rockford's place in baseball history did not end with Spalding and Barnes. In 1916, William Wrigley Jr., founder of the Wrigley Chewing Gum Company, bought a minority stake in the Chicago Cubs. Through a series of events and purchases, William became the sole owner of the Chicago Cubs by 1925. After William's death, his son P. K. (Philip Knight) became the leader of the Wrigley gum company and of the Chicago Cubs franchise. It was P. K. Wrigley who later founded the AAGPBL, baseball home of the Rockford Peaches. The Rockford Peaches won four league championships during the twelve AAGPBL seasons. They remain the most recognizable of the fifteen teams from the league.

The IWBC is in Rockford because one of the board members was in the right place at the right time. It stayed because of that sporting past and the community's dedication to preserving it. When Maybelle is asked why the IWBC chose an area of Rockford that had been forgotten for decades, she responds, "Where else would the center for women's baseball be but Rockford, home of the Peaches? We loved it there from our first visit. This is home."[5] With a physical location, and one already known for its love of baseball, Maybelle and Shirley had a new focus and renewed hope that there would one day be a place of their own.

On September 3, 2016, the IWBC was officially welcomed to Rockford with a dedication hosted by Winnebago County. Planned for the same time as the Peach Orchard Classic baseball tournament, former players of the AAGPBL, Maybelle Blair, Shirley Burkovich, Ange Armato, and Sis Waddell were on hand for the event, and stars from the movie *A League of Their Own* Anne Ramsey and Tracy Reiner also attended as the IWBC was officially welcomed to Rockford. Sitting on the stage alongside Shirley, Maybelle watched as one local celebrity or politician after another welcomed us to Rockford. A historian talked about the Peaches and their significance to the area and then, with a flourish, a twirl of her baseball-bat cane, Blair took the podium and the heart of Rockford.

With a combination of the wit and determination I had come to expect from her, Maybelle told the audience why the city should support the IWBC and our efforts to preserve the history of women in baseball. "We belong here, in the cradle of baseball. Who knows more about cradles than women?" She encouraged the girls who were there for the tournament to keep playing the game they loved and to always be proud of their history. "We support you because we know you love the game like we did. Keep playing. Never give up. Make a place for yourself and those younger than you." With old, dilapidated buildings still on the site and with very few people even knowing the IWBC existed, under the leadership of Maybelle and Shirley, the group accepted the buildings and the city's welcome, then set out to tell the world about the new home for women's baseball.

From 2016, when the IWBC first moved to Rockford, to March 31, 2022, Maybelle and Shirley led an organization from inception to success. Despite the accomplishments of the organization and Blair and Shirley's continued representation of the AAGPBL, a rift between them and the Players Association board continued, which frustrated and saddened Blair. The animosity was palpable. Just after the formation of the IWBC and the group's announcement that it was moving to Rockford, one former

All-American and a number of local Sarasota leaders announced they were going to build a women's sports museum in Florida. This would be for all sports and would honor all female athletes. They believed that people would travel to Florida but not to Rockford, Illinois. "No one wants to be there." In 2016, at the Sarasota reunion, Maybelle and Shirley were cornered and told by a former player and supporter of the Sarasota project that "you [IWBC] would never be successful. We are going to create another league of their own, build this big museum that would include, not focus on, women's baseball." Blair and Shirley were told to stop and join their efforts. That exchange both infuriated and inspired Maybelle and Shirley.

As they had done before when met with adversity, both Maybelle and Shirley used the exchange as motivation. They set out to connect with as much of the women's baseball world as possible. "We knew we needed to bring people into Rockford, and Shirley and I, with the help of Donna Cohen, connected to some people we already knew, like Justine Seigal, and a lot we didn't. It seemed to us that if we just started getting people to Beyer and to Rockford eventually, they would start to connect us with Rockford," Blair recalled. She was right. Due in equal parts to determination and hard work, the next year, 2017, the IWBC hosted the Baseball For All National tournament in Rockford, Illinois.

The night before the first tournament games, the IWBC hosted opening ceremonies at historic Beyer Stadium. In the outfield, each of the invited teams gathered behind their banners, in full uniform. By age, youngest to oldest, the teams walked along the third baseline toward home plate. Waiting on them were Maybelle Blair and Shirley Burkovich. Even the youngest, ten and under, were in awe of meeting Maybelle and Shirley. To a girl, they thanked them for paving the way. "Shirl and I were so shocked that those girls even knew who we were," Blair said. When Shirley asked some of the girls how they knew them, they started talking all at once. "We watch your movie all the time." "Our moms tell us how hard it was back in your time." "We want to be like you. Play like you." That experience was uplifting but, as Blair said, "Even that was nothing compared to watching those older girls play baseball on Beyer. Right there where the Peaches played in the 1940s." In 2017, two hundred girls, their coaches, and families brought girls' baseball back to Beyer. "Those girls were home," Blair said. "They were home."

They *were* home, a home created out of the dreams of Maybelle Blair. While Maybelle did not time her push to build a women's baseball home around the seventy-fifth anniversary of the AAGPBL, it happened that way, and the result was an even bigger splash. The year 2018 marked the seventy-fifth anniversary of the founding of the AAGPBL. The first game ever played by the AAGPBL was on May 30, 1943, and the first game ever played at Beyer Stadium was on June 3. The IWBC teamed with the city of Rockford and an army of volunteers to create a three-day celebration, which brought international attention and encompassed both important dates in women's baseball history. On May 30th, the IWBC hosted an AAGPBL celebration at the historic Coronado Theater in Rockford, which drew hundreds to the old theater.

In Rockford that weekend was Major League Baseball vice president and eventual general manager of the Marlins, Kim Ng, and other representatives of women's baseball. Maybelle, Shirley, and the former Rockford Peach Sis Waddel represented the AAGPBL. Ila Borders, the first woman to earn a scholarship for men's baseball, and members of a local women's baseball team were also on hand to celebrate the seventy-fifth anniversary of the AAGPBL and to help launch the IWBC and Rockford as the home of women's baseball. The entire three days were both celebratory and inspirational. The overwhelming success of the weekend also served as motivation for Maybelle. "This is great but only a beginning. We have to keep moving." She did. With the same tenacity with which she did everything else in her life, Maybelle gathered the goodwill and publicity garnered by the celebration and molded it into a springboard from which she could launch a movement. "We want to build a home for girls in baseball. Celebrate when they play. Make more opportunities for them to play." Incidentally, the celebration was scheduled to take place at the same time as the Women's Baseball World Cup. Both Maybelle and Shirley latched onto that coincidence and set out to use both events to further their goals for women's baseball.

The Women's Baseball World Cup is an international tournament in which national women's baseball teams from around the world compete. The inaugural Women's Baseball World Cup was chartered by the International Baseball Federation in 2002 and was held in Edmonton, Canada, in 2004. Before that tournament, the only other international women's baseball tournament was the Women's Baseball World Series. This was a smaller tournament and often included only three or four nations, usually Australia, Canada, Japan, and, occasionally, the United States. Before 2012, the tournament was sanctioned by the International Baseball Federation (IBAF). In 2013, the IBAF merged with the International Softball Federation, and subsequent tournaments have been sanctioned by the World Baseball Softball Confederation.

The World Cup includes teams from around the world and was hosted in many different countries, but, until 2018, it had never been played in the United States. At the same time that the IWBC was celebrating the past of women's baseball, the future was about to play in the United States for the first time. Each year, the host nation is allowed to have a trophy tour, culminating in the trophy's arrival at the World Cup site. At the seventy-fifth anniversary celebration of the AAGPBL, the IWBC was proud to kick off the first American national trophy tour. Standing on stage at the Coronado theater, as the trophy was unveiled, were three generations of women's baseball.

In August 2018, still as consistent as ever, Maybelle and Shirley were there to throw out pitches and to tell anyone who would listen about the IWBC. Held in the August heat of mid-coast Florida, the tournament was not well attended, and those who were there suffered, as did a number of players and umpires. At least one umpire fainted as a result of the heat. None of that deterred Maybelle and Shirley. They sat in the stands along-side movie director Francis Ford Coppola and watched some of the world's best baseball players take the field. Coppola was a sponsor of the Sonoma Stompers, who played in the Pacific Association of Professional Baseball Clubs. He was very supportive of the team's addition of two women, Kelsie Whitmore and Stacy Piagno. He was in Florida to see the best women's baseball had to offer in hopes of creating a coed baseball team. As he sat watching, Maybelle on one side and Shirley on the other, Coppola was bombarded with every reason why a coed team was not a good idea. The usually quiet Burkovich was adamant and animated when explaining why women needed their own league, not one with men. Maybelle was also firm in her attempt to convince Coppola to help create a women's league rather than a coed one. Ultimately, he did neither, but the experience of watching the World Cup with him was one that neither of them expected or forgot.

In hindsight, Blair thinks that the most important thing about that World Cup was the fact that there were women on the field in international competition. "I never thought I would ever see that happen. The crowd was small, and some teams needed a lot of work, but they were there. Then there was the Japanese team. They were great." She and Shirley encouraged the teams who struggled, sat in awe as they watched the Japanese team, and, openly and with admitted bias, cheered for the US team. They threw out a first pitch, visited the teams, and, despite language barriers, communicated respect, encouragement, and a shared love of the game.

In one of numerous interviews conducted with Blair about the seventy-fifth anniversary (of the AAGPBL) and the World Cup, she was very clear about the importance of those historic dates but adamant that it was the future of women's baseball that should be central to the celebrations. "We love to celebrate what we, the All-Americans did, but I am much more interested in how we can give these girls a chance to have what we had, a league of their own. That's really what we want. What I've always wanted. That's the reason this World Cup is so important, too. We are the past. That is the future." At those events and every one since, and at the urging of Maybelle, the IWBC uses the past to encourage the future.

It was Maybelle's mantra about connecting the past and the future that encouraged the IWBC to invite Baseball For All's National Tournament back to Rockford in that same year, 2018. Hosting the tournament in Rockford on Beyer Field during the seventy-fifth anniversary year was a physical manifestation of that goal. The ever-growing tournament saw its largest participation to date when over three hundred girls, their coaches, and their families attended the tournament. As they had done for every event planned by the IWBC, Rockford turned out for the games, encouraging the tournament to return to Rockford in 2019 for its third and final time. Even though the Nationals tournament has not been held in Rockford since 2019, following Maybelle's lead, the IWBC continues to sponsor the tournament every year.

8

STEPPING UP TO THE SPORT!

Penny Marshall, director of the movie *A League of Their Own*, died in December 2018. Steering all things women's baseball to Rockford, Maybelle thought that Marshall's celebration of life, and the dedication of a memorial to her, should be in Rockford. The timing was good because the IWBC had announced its plan to create an outdoor museum consisting of nine memorials dedicated to nine people, organizations, or groups that have been influential in women's baseball. Penny Marshall was the first of these honorees. In the summer of 2019, the design for her memorial was unveiled at an event held in her honor on Beyer Field. "It is fitting that Penny be remembered here, that her memorial be erected here, at the home of the Rockford Peaches," Blair claimed. "No one would have even known we existed if not for that movie. Now everyone knows." Simply designing a memorial to Penny was not enough, so Rockford rolled out the red carpet for the celebration.

To celebrate Penny Marshall, the IWBC hosted a series of events in September 2019. The kickoff was a Friday night VIP event, "Play Ball for Penny." The party was a 1940s Peaches-themed event. Marshall's daughter Tracy Reiner, her granddaughters, actresses Megan Cavanaugh, Anne Ramsey, and Patti Pelton, friends of Marshall, and local dignitaries made up a standing-room-only crowd. The next day, over four hundred people showed up at Beyer Field to honor the life of Penny Marshall and to witness the dedication of the IWBC's outdoor museum. As the crowd gathered, former AAGPBL players were escorted to their seats by members of the Little Peaches, a girls baseball team formed in Rockford, and players from the women's team, the Rockford Starfires. Three generations of girls and women who have played, and still play, baseball on Beyer Field.

After speeches by Major League Baseball Vice President Kim Ng, Congresswoman Cheri Bustos, Marshall's daughter Tracy Reiner, and former AAGPBL players, Madonna's song "This Used to Be My Playground" began to play. In what was a seminal moment in the life of the IWBC, we watched as one person after another slowly stood and began to sing along with Madonna, while Penny's daughter and granddaughters unveiled the memorial.

Neither Maybelle nor the IWBC stopped with that first design. The second memorial was unveiled in September 2020. Dedicated to the long history of African American women in baseball, this one featured Effa Manley, Lonnie Murray, Mone Davis, and many other women of color who have influenced the game. The third memorial was dedicated to the international game and featured teams and individual players, such as Japan's Ayami Sato. The fourth memorial highlights women umpires throughout history. Amanda Clements, Sophiyah Liu, and Perry Barber are among the women celebrated. Baseball writers and media were the focus of the fifth pylon, which featured Claire Smith, Dorothy Seymour Mills, and others. Furthering the quest to educate the public about the numerous ways women have been part of baseball, each year a new design is unveiled. The outdoor museum will stand as a physical manifestation of the long history of women in baseball.

Maybelle, excited about each new memorial design, celebrates every single one, but to her there is one major goal, an educational center and museum dedicated to women's baseball. The IWBC rests on three pillars: education, archives/museum, and on-field opportunities. While the organization has always thought that providing opportunities for girls to be part of baseball was important, education about the history, the struggles, and the successes was the most vital of the three pillars. Until very recently, most girls did not know they had a history in baseball, that they stand on the shoulders of amazing women. Teaching that history is crucial to them and to all of us who believe that "if you can't see it, you can't be it."

When talking about the history of women in baseball, Maybelle always discusses her own baseball history but also encourages her audience to think about and retell theirs. She believes that each of us has what amounts to a baseball creation story, a moment when we realize that we are the products of an illustrative history and not just an anomaly. It was at Blair's urging that I uncovered my own. Together we use it as an example to the current generation. Many years ago, a college professor asked me if I knew that women had played professional baseball. With a glint in her eye, she told me about a history I never read about in school. My history.

I responded with shock and disbelief. I spent hours locating newspaper articles and any other information I could find about this league. I read and reread the stories, and still I just could not believe it. If this was real, why hadn't someone told me before now? After all those years of pushing, of feeling alone, why? But with no way to fully understand this story, or why it had been kept secret, I tried to push it out of my mind once the class ended. Until July 4, 1992.

On that Saturday, I sat in a movie theater and watched, slack-jawed, as the very players I had read about played baseball on the screen. The movie *A League of Their Own* allowed me to see them, watch them play the game. I laughed and cheered when Geena Davis did the splits to catch a ball. I was outraged when she dropped the ball at home plate. But, mostly, I was in awe. At the end of the movie, the original ballplayers arrive in Cooperstown to play a softball game on Doubleday Field. I watched. Madonna started to sing, "This Used to Be My Playground," and I could no longer stop the tears. The credits began to roll. Madonna kept singing, and I couldn't move. Eventually the lights came up, and, startled, I looked up to see at least ten other women sitting in the theater. None of us could leave. If we did, then maybe they would go away. Maybe it wouldn't be real. But it was.

As a young adult sitting in that movie theater, I was introduced to my history for the first time. I learned I had a history and, yes, that mattered. If those women came before me, who came before them? Where is that history, and how do I fit into it? Even that tenuous connection to other female ballplayers gave me more confidence. The knowledge that, despite having had a pretty lonely childhood, I had always been part of this bigger team made me cry with relief, made me angry for the years I spent not knowing, and made me extremely grateful that I finally knew where I belonged.

"Yes," Blair said. "See, you found out and look what happened. Now you are sharing that history, preserving it, and using it to help girls. This is your life. That is why the IWBC is so important." She is correct. We must preserve, highlight, and use the history of women's baseball. Women's sporting history is not simply a set of artifacts to be viewed through glass or a collection of manuscripts tucked away in acid-free folders. Our history is alive, exciting, and relevant, and for the sake of us all we must use its vibrance. We must use that history to encourage the dreams of young girls, the intellectual ones and the physical ones. History can show girls who want to play that they are not alone and that the shoulders on which they stand are true, strong, and courageous. Those girls need to know that the foundation on which they stand is made up of some names we recognize and millions more that we don't. We want all children to know that those who came before them lift us up. They light our way to the pool, the court, and the field, and because of their strength we all have the gift of hope.

Baseball holds a special place in the collective hearts of many Americans and especially in Maybelle Blair's heart. She romanticized baseball's history and idealized former players. As a young girl growing up with the game, she mimicked the batting stance of her favorite players and pretended to be them when she played. Unlike many girls who loved the game but gave it up when they were discouraged from playing, Blair kept fighting just to play. For her and so many more, that fight is a fight for survival.

There is no doubt that women and girls who participate in sports are healthier, and there are hundreds of reports that point to the fact that participation in sports increases young women's self-esteem. Both rural and urban youths who play sports have lower dropout rates than do non-athletes, and those students who played high-school sports were more likely than nonathletes to describe themselves in favorable terms.[1] Girls and women who participate in sports, more often than others, define for *themselves* what it means to be a woman and the importance of success. Sport helps women realize that integrity, creativity, passion, and hard work are important elements of success and that true victory is defined long after the game is over. However, other benefits, such as increased confidence, independence, and leadership skills, are often less tangible and therefore overlooked. "Not by us," Blair says with force. "We get it. We know that showing those girls their history will make them stronger. We have to do that. Every day. On and off the field."

The IWBC relies on the educational arm of the organization to bolster the other two. Seeking new ways to bring women's baseball history to the fore, the IWBC partnered with the Society for American Baseball Research (SABR) to create the first Women in Baseball Conference. Now in its fifth year, the conference has brought in international participants and scores of people from around the United States to talk about women in all aspects of the game. From those panels, keynote talks, and discussions, girls and women from around the world learn about women's contributions, past and present. The result has been widespread understanding and discussion of women in baseball. Blair says, "I'm not going to sit and listen to people talk about baseball. I want to get out there and show people. But I'm glad others do it. It is so important to the girls." Because of the conference the IWBC has made contacts around the world, and it has used those to strengthen its foundation, education, and archives/museum components and, as Maybelle argues, "the best part of it all. Being on that field."

Most athletes, male or female, never reach the professional level. Yet nonprofessional athletes also realize benefits from participation in sports. For the most talented athletes, college scholarships and, ultimately, better preparation for employment translate into financial and professional rewards. For the rest of us, those who compete on local sandlots and in recreational leagues, the benefits may seem less tangible. But, by playing sports, individuals learn about teamwork, goal setting, and the critical skills necessary to succeed in the workplace. And another significant by-product of women's participation in sports is that young girls have an increasing number of female role models to emulate. Maybelle agreed, and, while her baseball heroes while she was growing up were all men, she is very glad that girls have an opportunity to see people who look like them on the field. "I didn't have posters on my wall like girls do today, but I did like certain players and wanted to play like them. They were my sports heroes." Due in part to the efforts of Maybelle and Shirley, among others, the very image of a successful athlete is being redefined. Women are now seen as sports stars, and the physical image of female athletes is now a familiar one to young girls. "That part is so important. God knows I don't want anyone to look like me or act like me, but I do want them to see we played and that a lot of girls played after us too."

There is a long line of women who played baseball, umpired, coached, or tended the fields after Blair's professional career. Each of them is important, but few were acknowledged or celebrated like those who formerly played in the AAGPBL were after 1992. Whether the IWBC was planning a conference, a tournament, or collecting historical documents for preservation, all of women's baseball history was highlighted.

The IWBC was the brainchild of former All-Americans Maybelle Blair, Shirley Burkovich, Karen Kunkel, and Jane Moffet. Due to her outgoing personality and the ill health of Moffet and Kunkel, Blair became the primary spokesperson of the group. As she had done in decades past and with other groups, Blair created a group of dedicated volunteers who believed, as she did, that girls deserve to play the greatest game on earth. "If they try to stop us, we will have something to say about it." She has a lot to say.

There was one other important event that the IWBC sponsored. Because of Maybelle's personality and her location near Hollywood, she was referred to Will Graham and Abbi Jacobson, writers of the Amazon Video series *A League of Their Own*, as a good resource for their show. Maybelle was interviewed by the writers and, as she normally does, she "hooked them. I just told them how it was and about things that most of the All-Americans didn't want to talk about. Even about my personal life. That's what they wanted to hear about, I guess. All of us think we were great ballplayers, and most weren't, so that same old song and dance gets old. I hooked 'em with other stories." Because Blair was such a hit early on, Shirley was pulled in as a consultant, as were others from the IWBC organization. From the relationship the writers, producers, directors, and actors had with Blair came a strong connection between the show, Amazon Video, and the IWBC, a connection that culminated in the premiere of the series being held in Rockford. That event was important not only to the IWBC but also to Maybelle Blair, personally, in a new adventure.

9

THE COMING-OUT

I sat up there on that stage, and my mouth flew open and out it came. Out I came.

Throughout her life, Maybelle Blair has overcome difficulty, heartache, and challenges. She has reveled in her successes, on and off a baseball field and as an advocate for women's baseball, and she has made great strides in the quest for equality. For decades, girls and women looked up to her for those efforts. Blair has thrown out too many first pitches to count, signed untold numbers of autographs, and sat for numerous interviews. Her story has been celebrated and respected, and girls loved being around her, but, after thirty years, it seemed that there was likely nothing new to share. Maybelle knew better, and she may have saved the most impactful piece of her story for her ninety-fifth year. With the headline, "She Inspired 'A League of Their Own.' At 95, She's Far from Done" the *New York Times* openly addressed an issue the movie *A League of Their Own*, and Maybelle herself, kept out of the spotlight: the same-sex relationships within the league. Products of their generation, the women of the AAGPBL never talked about sexuality and certainly not about homosexuality. Even today, eighty years later, the subject is taboo among many of the women who remain. Some argue there were "no lesbians in the league." Others have said, "Maybe a few but I didn't know them." Maybelle said, "Don't ask how many were. It would be easier to ask how many weren't. That was a well-kept secret, though." Sitting on a Tribeca Film Festival stage in 2022, Blair blew the lid off that badly kept secret.

The beloved Penny Marshall movie, which premiered in 1992, was very successful but was clearly a product of its time. Marshall could never have made a movie that even mentioned same-gender relationships, let alone highlighted those relationships within the league. The public rarely questioned that omission, and even those within the league were happy that part of their lives was not openly discussed. Among those same women, though, their relationships with each other and other women were simply part of their daily lives. Blair said, "Oh God, of course we all knew there were gay women in the league. Even those who weren't gay knew. And anyone who says different is not telling the truth. I think so many people wanted to protect the image of the league. Why? Maybe that would have been important in the 1950s, but why now?" Growing up in the 1930s and 1940s, women of the AAGPBL were aware of the grave consequences of being found out. It would have meant removal from the league and possibly even arrest. Keeping quiet about the women in their lives and even pretending to be in relationships with men were acts of survival during their playing days. Many, however, were never able to overcome the fear. They continued to keep their sexuality secret long after leaving the league. Even some of the women who were in relationships with other women continued to argue that there were never any "gay women" in the league. When asked about that claim, Maybelle simply burst into laughter.

The AAGPBL had no written rules that specifically addressed sexuality. Rather, they adhered to a policy much like the "gentleman's agreement" in Major League Baseball about race. The agreement was an unwritten policy that made it clear that no dark-skinned players were welcome. No written rule was needed. The AAGPBL used the same idea to keep the pristine image of mid-century American femininity on full display. In nearly every aspect of American society and culture, acceptable meant white, straight, middle class, and Christian. When Wrigley set out to create the league, he needed the talented softball players from around the Midwest but was aware of their image: manly, lesbian, unruly, decidedly not "all-American." Wrigley insisted that every girl or woman who tried out would meet his standard of acceptable femininity. Therefore, it was no accident that the league was called "All-American."

The league's use of socially constructed images and stereotypes was an age-old method of controlling women. Women were supposed to look and act in a certain way or face backlash from society. For women in the AAGPBL, if they did not conform to the league's idea of acceptable femininity, they faced expulsion from the league. Requirements included but were not limited to embodying a socially accepted definition of beauty. Players were expected to attend a charm school that was run by employees of the Helena Rubenstein Cosmetics company. For many Americans, including Wrigley, Helena Rubenstein represented the feminine ideal. He contracted with Rubenstein to create and teach the women a charm-school curriculum that included lessons on how to style their hair, apply makeup, and be ladylike in every situation, even on a ball diamond. Adherence to acceptable definitions of beauty was not limited to makeup or hairstyles, though; it also included the uniforms the players had to wear. Clad in short dresses, wearing makeup and having well-coiffed hair, AAGPBL players looked the epitome of American femininity. That image was only a visible manifestation of Wrigley's expectations. Many of the league's rules were unwritten and unspoken. The rules about race and sexuality were not written into the player handbook, but they were well known.

The narrative about and within the AAGPBL about race and sexuality is that neither women of color nor lesbians (if they stayed in the closet) were ever discriminated against. Clearly neither of those things was true. The popular mantra about Black women and the league is that "Black women just didn't try out." About lesbians it was, "Oh, there was none of that in the league." Neither of those things is true, and one reason we know that is that players like Terry Donahue and her partner of nearly seventy years, Pat Henchel, finally came out to the world. It took Maybelle Blair a little longer. It took decades and an Amazon television series, but she did it, onstage at the Tribeca Film Festival.

In 2019, director Will Graham, writer and actor Abbi Jacobson, and writer Liz Koe approached Blair about a new project they were working on, a version of *A League of Their Own* that explored the real lives of the women who played in the league. The three wanted the show to dig below the surfaces of race and sexuality and bring to the forefront truths that so many kept hidden for decades. Issues of race and sexuality were minefields during the 1940s and 1950s, and, like everyone else, members of the AAGPBL had to navigate those concerns carefully. Because those issues had not been discussed openly in the past, the creators of this new version of *A League of Their Own* were determined to bring that narrative to the public.

"A group of people wanted to do a TV show based on the league," Blair remembered, "I think it was Liz Koe who called me first and asked if she and Will could come down to visit and talk about it. Abbi was in New York at the time." Graham, the director of the extremely popular show *Mozart in the Jungle*, and Jacobson, the star of the acclaimed show *Broad City*, were unknown to Blair, as were their accomplishments. Blair told Koe, "Sure. I'm always glad to talk." The visit is a happy memory for Maybelle, not only because she became an integral part of making the series but also because of the relationships she formed with the group. "Those kids became my friends," Blair said. "I just love them, and I did from that first lunch we had."[1] Even now, five years after their first meeting, the actors, writers, and much of the crew still keep in touch with Maybelle.

The initial conversation was more about getting to know each other and the film people telling Blair about the project and how it was different from Penny Marshall's movie. "Liz and Will hinted around about being gay. And I didn't say too much about it. It's just not something I would bring up. So, mostly we just talked about the league." Maybelle is always excited when a new movie, book, podcast, or TV show features the players and the league. This time seemed different to her. It may have been the fact that she liked them personally or that they were young and she could sense their new enthusiasm, but whatever it was she remembered how happy and relieved she was when Liz called her again a few weeks later.

Liz called to ask if Blair would be willing to meet again and this time with Abbi as well. "I said, fine. I had no idea who Abbi was. They told me she's a big star and she's from New York. They came again and that time it was Will, Liz, and Abbi. I thought Abbi was the cutest thing because she was in jeans, and she had the cutest pair of boots. At that meeting they all told me they were gay. And asked about me. I said, yeah, well, you know, a little bit. They died laughing." Blair was right, "that first meeting was just different." That lunch changed the course of Maybelle's life and the lives of millions who watched the series. Blair still believes that the team of Will, Abbi, and Liz helped her far more than she ever helped them.

After taking time to get funding and hire producers and writers, the team called Maybelle again. This time it was to tell her that they were opening a studio and going forward with writing the show in preparation for selling it. "They asked me, and I asked Shirley to come to LA and talk about the league. All parts of it. Even the gay part. I said no problem and Shirley said, 'Well, I don't know anything about that! I can tell them about the league, but not that other stuff.'" Shirley and Maybelle went to Los Angeles to be interviewed by the team. For both, the experience was exciting and fun. For Maybelle, it was liberating. "We walked into this room. And there was, oh my God, I've never seen so many writers in my life. They got us up there and started questioning us like we were on trial or something, and it was sort of fun. They asked a million questions, and then they got around to asking me about being gay." Blair remembers fumbling a bit with her answer. After ninety years of hiding, of pretending and avoidance, it was strange to be asked the question so openly and in front of so many people. She finally said, "Yes, I'm gay." Not knowing what was going to come of the project or her friendship with the team, she answered their questions but with an edge of caution.

Will, Abbi, and Liz felt much the same way Maybelle did about their friendship. The four grew close, and as a result Blair opened up more about her life in and out of the AAGPBL. "They wanted to know what our lives were like away from the field too, which was different from most people who interviewed me or other players." Since the movie was released in 1992, the former players have been interviewed, photographed, and written about over and over but never about their personal relationships. It was a glaring omission, but until Will, Abbi, and Liz dared to broach the subject, the players themselves were content to keep that part of their lives secret. "We were all so afraid to talk about the gay stuff and even all these years later we were worried about the league. What would they, the other ball players, think of us? Isn't that stupid?" While that level of fear might seem silly now, for women of that generation, the fear of scorn, abandonment, and ostracization was very real, even in the twenty-first century.

It took time for Maybelle to articulate what her life was like in the 1940s and 1950s. Eventually, though, Maybelle recalled, "I opened my mouth and out it all came. All of it." The writers were interested in personal stories about what they did. Were there gay bars, and did they sneak around and go meet girlfriends or girls from the towns where they lived? "Oh yes, all of that," Maybelle said with a laugh. "I told them all about us sneaking out after curfew and going to local bars and how a lot of us had crushes on one another. Some stories I probably shouldn't have told." Some of those stories, such as those about relationships with other players and the bar raid at the IF Club, made it into the series. Parts of other stories were used as a foundation for the Amazon series writers' own creativity. As Maybelle continued to trust them and talk more about her time in the league and how it influenced her personal relationships, she waffled back and forth between feeling energized, free, and scared. "I even said to Abbi one time, my God, I'm going to be pushed out of the All-Americans for sure. They've been trying to do that for years and now they will do it all the way." Blair made that comment with some levity, but the anxiety about being found out, about telling those stories in public to a group who wanted to put it on a TV screen, dominated her thoughts.

As Blair thought would happen, members of the AAGPBL Players Association were furious with her for being so open about those personal stories. When they were interviewed by Will and Abbi, they gave a completely different view of life in the league. Maybelle estimated that at least 60 to 70 percent of the players were gay, but when representatives of the Players Association were asked to estimate the number of women in same-sex relationships, they said, "Oh, there were no gay women in the league at all." Maybelle reacted to that comment with outrage. "It's so stupid, you know, they think they are protecting the league. It's not protecting the league. It's actually what happened. The league does not need to be protected. It was 80 years ago, what are they protecting them from?" For years Blair went along with the silence. But once she started telling her story and hearing the Amazon series writers' positive feedback, she became even more determined to tell her truth. After all, the show was only in the hands of writers at that point. It was unclear whether it would even get picked up by a studio.

The time between her interviews with the team and the next step seemed like years to Blair and Shirley. The two of them continued to travel and represent women's baseball and the IWBC wherever they could. And they waited. Maybelle and Shirley were told that selling the show would be time-consuming, but they had all but given up when Blair got a call. "I answered the phone and all I hear is, 'Babe we sold it.' I said 'You're kidding.' And then they all started screaming." Blair remembered how excited she was to get that call. "The first thing that went through my mind was 'Wow, that is so great.' But the second thing was, 'Uh oh. Now you've done it, Blair.'"

The wheels were in motion, and the next step was to get the first episodes filmed. At first the show filmed scenes in Los Angeles. The team invited Shirley and Blair to come and be part of the filming. Some of the All-Americans who lived in the area showed up to watch and be part of the fun. The show was on its way and so was Maybelle's renewed popularity. But never satisfied and always pushing for the next field, team, or baseball opportunity, Maybelle insisted that the show should be filmed in Rockford. Benefiting both the city of Rockford and the IWBC, filming a portion of the show at the actual home of the Peaches became a new goal for Blair. The IWBC helped by reaching out to Illinois state legislators, city government officials, and the state tourism department. Unfortunately, state taxes were much higher in Illinois than in other places, so most of the show ended up being filmed just outside Pittsburgh. Up to the actual premiere of the show, Maybelle was pushing for "just one scene" to be filmed in Rockford. It never was.

Blair wasn't happy about the location, but, when she and Shirley were invited to visit the sets in Pennsylvania, they jumped at the chance. "They were building the sets and everything. Oh my gosh, we saw the ballpark before it got fixed. It was half up and half down, and they showed us how they cut a bus in half, cut the top off so they could film in it. I'd never seen such a thing." Production of the show's full run of eight episodes took longer than Blair realized it would, but, in early 2022, she and a few others from the IWBC were allowed to preview the first episode. Anxious for her opinion and aware of Maybelle's lack of computer skills, Abbi and Will brought a laptop computer to Blair's house for her own private viewing.

Blair was excited to see the show but was unhappy with a couple aspects of the first episode. "I thought that one thing I would have changed is the swearing. We never swore in the All-Americans. I don't think I heard anybody say anything but maybe damn or that type of thing. But none of the girls at that time swore like they did in the show." As with all shows, the creators and writers of this one made decisions based on what they thought would appeal to an audience. The other piece she resisted was the way they had Rosie O'Donnell and others dressed, "all dykey." "I told them we did not dress like that. Maybe girls in New York or Los Angeles, but I didn't know it. And in our league and where we were, the girls dressed like women." Lesbian dress in the 1940s and 1950s varied, depending on class, region, and race. In working-class bars, women were more likely to dress in a style Blair saw as "too butchy." More upscale bars saw women dressed in dresses and wearing makeup.[2] Maybelle's gay-bar experience varied, but to her it was important that women looked like women. "If I wanted a man, I'd go out with a man. The way they showed Rosie, a suit, chains, boots. That was not common." Naturally, Blair's experience was her own. She did not frequent the same bars, socialize at the same parties, or seek out women who looked masculine. So, in her experience, those women were not prevalent. While she may not have been happy about the cursing or the masculine representation of some of the women in the show, that fact did not keep her from being proud of the show or from traveling with the show's team to promote it.

Between the final filming and the beginning of the travel to publicize the show, Shirley Burkovich died, leaving Blair alone to carry on their mission and the promotion of the new version of *A League of Their Own*. The loss of Shirley stunned and saddened Maybelle. But it also inspired her to do more and to do it faster. Once the show was finally ready for release in the late summer of 2022, Amazon representatives and the team, which now included actors Chanté Adams, Gbemisola Ikumelo, and D'Arcy Carden, set off across the country to publicize it. The most exciting opportunity came when the Tribeca Film Festival, known simply as Tribeca, accepted the show's first episode into its 2022 festival. The annual festival is organized by Tribeca Productions and takes place each spring in New York City. It was founded by Robert De Niro, Jane Rosenthal, and Craig Hatkoff in 2002 to help encourage economic and cultural revitalization of Lower Manhattan after the September 11, 2001, attacks on the World Trade Center. Each year, the festival hosts over six hundred screenings with approximately one hundred fifty thousand attendees. It awards independent artists in twenty-three juried categories.[3] Maybelle remembered that she got a call asking if she could go to New York for "some film festival. I had never heard of it, but they told me it was a big deal to be invited so I got excited too." In what would be the biggest event she had participated in since Shirley's death, Blair went to New York, missing her friend but glad that this thing they started together was finally happening.

Immediately after the show premiered, there was a public conversation with Abbi Jacobson, Will Graham, Executive Producer Desta Tedros Reff, cast members Chanté Adams, D'Arcy Carden, and Gbemisola Ikumelo, and Maybelle Blair. In hindsight, Blair says the panel started like many others she had been part of over the years. "The group talked about making the show, how much fun it was, and how they respected the players for what they did. You know, the same old routine." This was not like any other show, however, and was anything but another baseball story.

Because Will and Abbi and other members of the cast and crew were openly gay, and because they freely talked about their own sexuality, Blair opened up too. "As you know, I was so scared about people knowing so I didn't really talk too much about it. That night, they were sitting there on that stage, talking, and I finally said to myself, 'If those kids [Will, Abbi, etc.] out here are gay, if they can come out and tell that they're gay, why can't I come out and help?' Maybe some other kids wouldn't have to go through what I had to go through. 'I'm old enough,' I thought. So, I opened my mouth and said it." What she said was,

> These young girl ballplayers need to realize that they're not alone and you don't have to hide. I can see their struggles in those little eyes. I hid for seventy-five, eighty-five years, and well maybe it's time. This is actually, basically, the first time I've ever come out.

After several minutes of a standing ovation, Maybelle "kept thinking, sit down. Okay. Okay. The more they clapped, the more worried I got. I kept thinking, well, I guess this was a big deal. Maybe at ninety-five, it won't be so bad. Maybe your family won't disown you. Rod and Marlene and the boys, I don't want them to disown me. So, after I said some of that stuff I got scared."

Blair need not have worried about her family. Her beloved nephew Rod said of Blair's coming-out, "In baseball, we have an expression when you're playing well or you're playing poorly. All you do is say, 'next pitch.'" He expressed love and support for his aunt and praised her courage. "For her to say verbally, say what she did out loud was necessary to go forward and I think it's made her life better. I mean, there's no question in my mind." As is often the case with families, they knew she was gay. All they wanted to do was to reassure her that "that stuff doesn't matter. She's just Aunt to us."[4]

Later that night, after the premiere, the group attended an after-party where Maybelle was overwhelmed with well-wishers and people telling her how proud they were of her. "Everybody was coming up to me, telling me how much it meant to them that I said that, and then this lady walks up to me and she says, 'I'm so proud of you' and all of this and that. Turns out that was Jen Salke, head of Amazon Studios. You know me, I told her all about the IWBC and how we were building a museum." Even during her own fifteen minutes of fame and glory, she was working.

The weeks and months after her coming-out in New York were full of interview requests, podcast and television appearances, and exposure to a whole new audience. "I never thought this would get so much attention, but I was glad because then I could let all these little girls and little boys know that they are not alone. And it's okay to come out and don't hide your feelings towards people." Until she became friends with Will, Abbi, Liz, Jamie Babbit, and other crew members and actors from the show, Maybelle continued to live in a world influenced by her mid-twentieth-century sensibilities about sexuality. "They talked so open about being gay and about their stories. They use 'queer.' I don't like that word, so I say gay. But they just opened the book up for me. 'Tell me about your gay life,' they said. I did, slow at first because I was afraid, then I just said it all." While Blair's coming-out was therapeutic for her personally, it was one more step into what had been a life of building opportunities. To her, those conversations were important to the TV show, a way for them to get the full stories of the league, but, to the young people who witnessed the courage it took for her to come out publicly at age ninety-five, it was life altering. Wherever she went, people who already knew her, and even more who didn't, approached Blair to congratulate her and to thank her. As she was being pushed in a wheelchair through the Chicago airport, a kid stopped her to say how much he appreciated what she did. That young man was neither a baseball player nor did he have a particular interest in the game. He needed his own version of a runway, someone braver than he was to show him the way. As she had done for decades within baseball, she created a path for him and scores of others.

Coming out was like a beginning, according to Blair, but it also sparked a reexamination of her life. Knowing and understanding her sexuality was not new to Maybelle, but she admits that, after coming out, she started remembering more and really thinking about all those years of crushes and fear. "It's like I never really let myself think about all that stuff. Maybe it was too hard." Maybelle claims that she always knew she was gay. "Even when I was a little girl. I realized I was different." As early as the sixth grade, Maybelle had a crush on her teacher. "You know, I thought I was almost in love with her. I just loved her. You know, I didn't know what love was, but I just thought she was the greatest thing that ever lived. I could hardly wait to get to school just to see her." Looking back, she realizes that her feelings were likely admiration and not love, but Blair still remembers the feelings that teacher aroused in her and how ashamed she felt about them. "That didn't stop me, though," Maybelle said with a laugh. "It wasn't too much after that time that I met my next love."

Each spring Maybelle's elementary school took some students on a visit to the local high school, showing them where they would be going, and giving them a tour. "They showed us the auditorium. I've never seen anything like it. It was huge, to me anyway. We went in there, looking around and up there on the stage was this girl. She was a cheerleader. God, she was absolutely the prettiest thing I had ever seen." Even after that experience Maybelle remembered that, "while I knew I felt something, I didn't know what it was. Was it admiration, or did I fall in love? I don't know what happened, but boy oh boy." At the time she was unable to fully understand her feelings or to recognize them in others.

It was the same school year that several of Blair's classmates began telling her that another student "really loves you." Confused, Maybelle said, "What are you talking about?" "No," they said. "Really, she is in love with you. Look, she wears the same clothes as you." As if to prove their claims, the kids pointed out how Blair's admirer had a dress made just like Maybelle's. "My mother made this blue dress with white daisies on it. About a month after I wore that dress, here she came with the same dress. I don't think that meant she loved me, but my classmates kept saying it." That experience and the memory of it are less confusing now. Back then, hearing kids say those things out loud was terrifying to Maybelle. She neither understood nor wanted to understand them. In hindsight, she knows why: those jeers from classmates were too close to the truth, a truth even she did not recognize.

By the time Maybelle entered high school, she had a much better idea what was going on so, when she met Helen, the girl who she admits was her first love, the excitement was mixed with fear, anxiety, and a constant worry about being discovered. Blair's relationship with Helen was what Blair called "her first episode," and, while it didn't last past high school, Maybelle now believes that her early relationship may have been one of the most important in her life. She was not aware of it then, but Maybelle now thinks that having a positive experience took some of the fear away and that made it possible to keep being herself. Much of this insight about her early life is a new experience for Maybelle and, according to her, a direct result of her own eyes being opened by Will, Abbi, and the team.

Until that night in New York, most of Blair's life was about creating opportunities for herself and for other girls and women in baseball. That quest continues, but, because of her own personal awakening, Maybelle realized that young people struggle for acceptance in a lot of ways and not all of them are connected to sports. "After that night in New York I thought a lot about my life and how hard it was when I was young. God, why would I want kids to have to do that now? Maybe I can help." For Maybelle and likely a lot of other girls, there was a connection between sports and their sexuality, but it is often just too hard to recognize. Playing a sport often provides a place where girls can be athletic, aggressive, wear pants, and act out aspects of themselves that are unacceptable off the field. It never occurred to Maybelle that those parts of her life were so intricately connected. Once she realized it, though, openness and honesty about all aspects of her journey became as important as building one more baseball diamond.

Blair was energized and had a new purpose, and the success of the show became paramount to her. She traveled around the country with Will and Abbi to preview the show and to publicize its importance. Always loyal to Rockford and the IWBC, she pushed to have a big premiere party in Rockford. The producers of the show may not have been able to film the show in Rockford, but they were willing to throw a big viewing party there. "It seemed important to have something in Rockford, important to the people there and to the show. A lot of people, mostly All-Americans, were not happy with the sex stuff when they saw it, so in order to keep the league and the Peaches connected, I thought we should have a big ol' street party." Whether it was for the reasons Blair mentioned or their desire for publicity, Amazon representatives agreed.

At Maybelle's urging, the studio planned a huge blowout in Rockford, all centered around a showing of the pilot episode of *A League of Their Own* at the city's historic theater, the Coronado. On the street in front of the theater, dancers in 1940s dress, cars from the era, and baseball-themed refreshments brought thousands to downtown Rockford. In addition to Abbi and Will, actors D'Arcy Carden and Chanté Adams and Executive Producer Desta Tedros Reff attended the event. The actors, along with Maybelle, walked a green, not red, carpet into the Coranado. A sellout crowd watched the first episode. They cheered the first time the Rockford Peaches were mentioned and erupted into hoots and applause when Maybelle and Shirley appeared on the screen in their cameo. The studio continued to take the first episode and Maybelle around the country.

In August 2022, the twenty-first-century version of *A League of Their Own* premiered on Amazon. The show was extremely popular and almost immediately led to a very dedicated and vocal fandom. Naturally, reviews compared the show to Penny Marshall's 1992 film, but few criticized the show for not being true to Marshall's film; rather, they praised the creators for their courage and creativity. Kevin Fallon of *The Daily Beast* said, "Abbi Jacobson and Will Graham's reimagining of Penny Marshall's 1992 classic film is the rare case of creators understanding exactly what made a story special and expanding the world in a valuable, fascinating way."[5] And NPR wrote, "It may not be precisely what fans of the film expect, but it stands on its own as a story about finding avenues of freedom within worlds that remain disappointingly limiting."[6]

Similarly to real life, not everyone agreed with having an open discussion about sexuality and certainly not when it made their baseball heroes look anything but wholesome. Despite the production team's efforts to honestly tackle the issues of sexuality and race within the AAGPBL, critics and some Amazon viewers relied on familiar homophobic messages to attack the show. In attempts to lower the approval ratings, many one-star reviews flooded the Amazon website. Most of the negative reviews pointed to the show's LGBTQ+ representation as their primary reason for the low score. One review read, "This is ridiculous. I had to turn it off. Everyone in the show is a lesbian. I thought I was going to be watching something good. I was wrong." Another reviewer wrote, "A league of inspirational women breaking barriers or a league of sexually confused lesbian women?"[7] Blair admitted that she expected a lot of those comments, but, arguing that it was past time that the women from that league, who clearly had influence on girls and women, began using that influence in important ways, she brushed them off.

Maybelle sincerely believed that she and the other women from the league had a responsibility to be honest about their lives so that a younger generation of girls would never have to be afraid to come out, but she never expected that women who were openly gay would also be so impacted.

"While I was afraid of what my family would say and all that, I didn't think the women and girls I had gotten to know over the years would be affected at all." Using Ila Borders as an example, Blair talked excitedly about how the women who already knew she was gay and who were gay themselves reacted to the show and to Blair's involvement. Borders was the first woman to be a starting pitcher during a men's collegiate baseball game. Years later, in 2017, her biography, *Making My Pitch: A Woman's Baseball Odyssey*, cowritten with Jean Ardell, was published. In the book, Borders documents her own struggles in playing baseball and in being a lesbian. "She always knew about me, but I swear to God, since the show and my coming-out, she loves me and won't stop kissing me!" Maybelle said with a laugh. "Oh, and Alvarez [Veronica Alvarez is the manager of the USA Women's Baseball Team]. We were always close but now we are even closer. I did not realize how that would happen, how even those who knew would get closer." Maybelle credits the TV show with these positive changes in old friendships and the creation of new ones. Arguing that she would have continued to live as she had for ninety-five years if not for the show, Maybelle admits that she will be forever grateful to Will and Abbi for helping to make this part of her life possible, and for helping to make it possible for new generations.

Despite an all-out push from the show's fandom, which included hiring a small plane to pull a support banner over the studio, the Amazon version of *A League of Their Own* was not renewed for a second season. Cries of homophobia and racism from fans were loud and angry but did nothing to change the studio's decision. The cancellation was a disappointment to Maybelle because she believed that, if the show continued, it would keep the IWBC in the public eye and continue to help younger generations of kids struggling with coming out. Despite her efforts to contact friends at Amazon Studios and her pleas in the media for another season, season two of the show was not produced.

In the two years after the show premiered and Blair came out on that New York stage, the divide between Maybelle and the AAGPBL deepened, but that did not stop her from attending their yearly reunions. "I'm an All-American too, and I will go as long as I'm able." Nor did that negativity slow her quest to build a home for women's baseball or damage her reputation with the public. "That could have ended me," she said of the coming-out. "It didn't and you know what? I survived." Admittedly, sometimes she still has to fight the ingrained fear of being "found out," but the difference now, Blair points out, is that "it's okay. What does it matter? I'm me and because I said what I did a few others will be able to as well. That is important, almost as important as baseball," Blair said laughing. Rethinking, she said, "Well, maybe."

Once she felt fully connected to the show, Maybelle employed the same tenacity that she used to create teams and ball diamonds for herself and others to help ease a path to acceptance. She swallowed the fear of being found out and kept moving forward. Whether it was riding on an old gate while her brother drove around the makeshift baseball diamond, demanding that her middle school form a team for girls, creating teams at her places of employment, or heading off to Chicago on her own to play professionally, Maybelle Blair was brave, demanding, and constantly creating opportunities for herself and others. Talking openly about her sexuality is perhaps the bravest thing she's ever done, and it may have the longest-lasting impact. Whether it does or not, embracing that part of her life and going public with the untold story of the AAGPBL gave Maybelle Blair new focus and a whole new set of reasons for fans to admire her determination and to benefit from the pathways to success and personal happiness she helped to build.

CONCLUSION

Well, I'm not dead yet. Why are you writing a conclusion?

For decades Maybelle Blair has willingly shared her personal baseball story with anyone who will listen. She has been the topic of documentaries, articles, and chapters of books about the league, and she even became an LGBTQ+ icon. Despite all that, she does not think of herself as someone worthy of a legacy. Whenever I asked her, "What do you want your legacy to be?" she was usually vague and dismissive. "Legacy" is not a word Blair would ever use in relation to herself. She has consistently resisted the idea that she is a role model. She repeatedly points out that she was not a superstar and only played with the All-Americans for a year. Her time playing softball and her short All-American career did not, in her mind, qualify her as someone worthy of having a legacy.

"Legacies are things people have who have done something," Blair says. If playing for the All-Americans was her only contribution to women's baseball then, she might be right. But, of course, it isn't. The common theme of her life is as follows: never take no for an answer, and always say yes to an opportunity. When she was a child, her brother and father taught her the game of baseball and, albeit in a peripheral way, gave her a way into the game, first as a weight on the old gate used to drag the field and later as an outfielder running down fly balls for her brother. As an elementary-school student, she was outraged when the boys got to travel to other schools to play ball and the girls couldn't. She was not going to accept that slight so, with the help of a teacher, Maybelle put together a team of girls, and off they went to challenge teams at other schools. To her, none of that made her worthy of having a legacy, let alone inspiring a book.

In her early twenties, Maybelle joined traveling softball teams that entertained the military personnel at bases along the West Coast. Later she was recruited to play professional softball in Chicago and then for the AAGPBL. Still, to her, none of that warranted having a legacy. During her Northrop career, she formed teams for both men and women, and, once she retired, Maybelle turned her focus to preserving the memory of women in baseball. In 2014, Maybelle and Shirley Burkovich along with former players from the AAGPBL Karen Kunkle, Jane Moffet, and Mary Moore, working together with Donna Cohen and me, created the IWBC. The organization's very existence is about women's baseball, the preservation of it, and the support of those who want to play. Nor was the formation of the IWBC enough to justify having a legacy in Maybelle's mind.

When I pointed out to her how, at each of the phases of her life, she was either playing, building diamonds out of nothing, or creating opportunities for others to play, she responded with a slight cock of her head and a characteristically Maybelle Blair comment, "Okay, I guess I did do those things. I'll take a legacy." Taken as a whole, Blair's life in and around baseball and softball is her legacy and our gift. She is the first to say that none of that would have happened without scores of other people, her family, and the hundreds of teammates she had over the years. Maybelle had a desire to be part of a game, and along the way that game became life for her. Through the twists and turns of life, baseball was the one constant. It gave her hours of entertainment and feelings of accomplishment during difficult times. The baseball field became a place where she experienced peace and comfort. And the world that swirled around those diamonds became one where Maybelle Blair created relationships and a legacy.

Blair's life must be examined in the context of America's baseball story and within the socially constructed definitions of gender, class, and sexuality. Doing so helps us to better understand baseball history as a whole. By using the lenses of gender and sexuality, we can examine the importance of the game to American women. To understand the long-term impact of playing baseball on the lives of girls and women, we should also examine the intersection of their lives and baseball, the location where the two meet. Maybelle's story helps us to do just that. Her story could focus on her successes on the playing field or be used as an example of a woman who triumphed in a male-dominated world. It could tell us about the often-scary world of gays and lesbians and the effects of war on women in the United States during the twentieth century. None of these perspectives, however, limited as they are to the traditional lenses of gender, sexuality, and class, provides us with the complete picture, the full arc of Maybelle's life. It is the whole story, the determination, and the dedication to baseball, baseball for everyone, that makes Blair's story worthy of retelling.

When I finished writing this book, I looked back again at Maybelle Blair's life—not just the narrative of her life, the triumphs and the tragedies, and not just the baseball—but the full arc of it. I laughed for the millionth time at some of her antics, felt sad when she lost the love of her life and was proud when she blew the door off the closet at Tribeca. Her life as a whole and those events individually inform us about a time period and inspire us never to give up on a dream. But what did it all mean to Maybelle? What did she want us to take away from her story? I asked her what she wanted us, her friends, fans, and family, and the young girls who are fighting to play baseball to learn from her life. "Well," she said, as she put her hand on her chin as if to think of something to say, "Now, that's not a quick answer. Sit down. This may take a while." It did, but her insights were well worth the time.

First, Blair listed the things we all say when we are talking to someone who is younger than we are, "Be yourself. Don't let anyone tell you that you can't do something. Enjoy each day. They go by so fast." While she continued talking, often in a circular fashion, I began to see the threads unravel. As she often did, Maybelle relied on baseball to explain herself. What follows is my interpretation of her answer to the question, "What is your charge to us?"

Baseball is like life. You start at home, and you end up back at home, right where you started. It's not just an uninterrupted jog around the bases, though—unless you hit a home run; most of us can't do that. Remember to touch all the bases on your journey. When you need to, run fast, not from things, but to them. Second base, third base, home. When you get winded or an opposing player is about to tag you, stop your progress, wait. Stay on your base. But always be alert. Never stop looking for a chance to go again. When the next player hits the ball and the moment comes for you to move on, don't hesitate. Do it. You might be thrown out, or you might score. In the long run it doesn't matter which. When the play is over, you'll be home, no matter what. Whether you scored a run or not, celebrate as you head to your dugout. You were in the game.

As Blair nears ninety-eight years of age, she still looks ahead as much as she looks back. "What can we do now? What if we host this tournament, sponsor this girls' team?" But in her urging of us to "move," to do more, raise more money, and do it faster, Maybelle not only shows that she feels the press of time but also demonstrates to the rest of us that every day, every year should be lived. There is never a time in one's life when we should simply stop living and rest on our laurels. There is no age when we can step back and say, "Okay, your turn now." If you have a dream, live it. If you have a goal, achieve it, and, if you are fortunate enough to live into your nineties, remember what Blair says when people ask how she does so much at her age, "No day should be wasted. I still have a lot to do while I'm on this side of the grass." With that quote in mind, I wondered, is it even possible to write a conclusion to a biography about Maybelle Blair? Can we sum up her life, her achievements, her failures, and her impact on baseball and the lives of so many? I'm not sure we can. The pages of this book simply cannot contain the energy and the zest for life or the love of baseball that flows from her, even at ninety-seven. There is no conclusion, not yet.

ACKNOWLEDGMENTS

This book would not exist without Maybelle Blair, but not just for the obvious reason. Yes, it is her story, but, as she has done for over twenty years, Blair encouraged, nudged, and supported me as I slowly (too slowly for her) proceeded through this project. She managed to navigate the fine line between wanting me to do the book and not fully believing she was worthy of it. She is. And, no matter how readers view the book, it will never do her justice. For the two decades of friendship, for the love and support, and for allowing me to be a spectator to and a beneficiary of your life, thank you.

Greta Rensenbrink, my spouse and my best friend, made this book possible in so many ways. From reading drafts, editing, taking over household chores and dog walks, and providing countless pep talks, she poured herself into this book. Her love, support, and confidence in the project were crucial to its completion.

From supporting my projects, including this book, to traveling, flying in antique planes, zip-lining, and other adventures, my sister has always been by my side. Her courage and spirit are crucial to all I do.

My mom and dad were the first ones to teach me about baseball, the excitement of it, the highs and the lows and the absolute joy of playing it. For that early introduction to baseball, I thank them.

My ever-growing baseball family continues to encourage me in everything I do. I thank them for the support and friendship. A few individuals from that group need to be singled out. Leslie Heaphy and Ryan Woodward have given me friendship, advice, and encouragement above and beyond. To you both, thank you.

I have missed Shirley Burkovich every day since her passing on March 31, 2022. She was the best of us all. Honest, kind, forgiving, and loyal. On days when I am overwhelmed or discouraged, the example she set gives me courage and hope. Thank you, Shirl.

Christen Karniski from Rowman & Littlefield was encouraging from the beginning and has been insightful and patient. Working with her has made this project much easier.

APPENDIX

Timeline of Women in Baseball

The information below comes from the National Baseball Hall of Fame, https://baseballhall.org/women-in-baseball.

"We've always been part of the game. No one seems to know that. Show them the proof." With that charge from Maybelle, I set out to create the timeline below. It is not complete. A full discussion of the roles and accomplishments of girls and women in the game of baseball would take volumes to fully explore. This list is only a sampling meant to illustrate the longevity and the diversity of women's participation in the sport.

★★★

1866:	The first organized team of women players was formed when Vassar College, then an all-women's college, started its first baseball team called the Vassar Resolutes. The team was forced to disband in 1878 because of parents' concerns over the safety of baseball for their daughters.
1890s:	"Bloomer Girls" baseball teams barnstormed the United States from the 1890s to 1934, playing local town, semipro, and minor-league men's teams.
1898:	Lizzie Arlington became the first woman to play on a men's professional team, the Philadelphia Reserves. Later she played for the minor-league team, the Reading Coal Heavers.
Early 1900s:	At the age of seventeen, Alta Weiss joined a men's semiprofessional team, known as the Vermillion Independents. She used the money earned through baseball to attend college. Eventually, she went to medical school and became a doctor.

1904:   Amanda Clement, then sixteen years old, became the first female professional umpire in baseball. She left baseball in 1910 and also used the money earned playing baseball to pay for her college education.

1911:   Helene Britton became the first female owner of a major-league team when she inherited the St. Louis Cardinals after the death of her uncle. Britton remained the owner of the Cardinals until 1918.

1920:   After seventy-two years of fighting, the Nineteenth Amendment, allowing women to vote, was finally ratified. This political victory, along with a period of social and political change, led to the creation of a number of women's baseball teams around the country.

1925:   The Philadelphia Bobbies, an all-women's baseball team, including Edith "The Kid" Houghton, traveled to Japan in hopes of barnstorming the country. After the promoters of the trip pulled out, the trip ended in tragedy with the loss of one player.

1931:   Sixteen-year-old Jackie Mitchell signed a contract with a men's minor-league team, the Chattanooga Lookouts. The Lookouts staged an exhibition game against the New York Yankees, arranging for Mitchell to pitch against Babe Ruth and Lou Gehrig. The story is that Mitchell stuck out both Ruth and Gehrig. One week later, Commissioner Landis ruled that Mitchell's contract was null and void, beginning a ban of women players that lasted until 1993.

1935:   Effa Manley and her husband Abe purchased the Brooklyn Eagles, a Negro Leagues franchise that eventually moved to Newark. Effa Manley ran the business operations of the Eagles, managing the payroll and negotiating contracts with the players. After Abe's death, she owned the team. Effa is the only woman who has been inducted into the National Baseball Hall of Fame.

1943:   Chicago Cubs owner Philip Wrigley, concerned about the negative impact of World War II on baseball, formed the All-American Girls Professional Softball League. The league soon switched to baseball and became known as the All-American Girls Professional Baseball League (AAGPBL). The league lasted from 1943 to 1954. Nearly six hundred women played during the twelve years of the league's operation.

1952:   Eleanor Engle signed a contract with the Harrisburg Senators, a Philadelphia A's affiliate. Shortly after she signed her contract, minor-league president George Trautman and Major League Baseball Commissioner Ford Frick voided it. The incident led to warnings that both major- and minor-league teams that tried to sign women would be punished.

1953–1955:   Three women played in the Negro Leagues for the KC Monarchs and Indianapolis Clowns: Toni Stone, Connie Morgan, and Mamie

Johnson. Johnson attended a tryout for the AAGPBL in Alexandria, Virginia, in the early 1950s. Because it was segregated, the AAGPBL did not allow her to try out.

1955: Bill Allington formed two women's teams called Allington's All-Stars, which barnstormed the United States, playing men's town and semipro teams. Many of his players had just begun to play for the AAGPBL when it ended and took this opportunity to continue playing baseball.

1962: Joan Payson became the owner of the expansion New York Mets. She was the first female owner to buy a team with her own money and not inherit it from a male family member.

1969: Bernice Gera signed a professional umpiring contract. The idea of becoming an umpire came to her when she began to see umpiring games in slums as "a form of social welfare." She thought that having a woman on the field would lead to "less trouble" and would encourage other women to attend the games. Despite her experience and success, the National Association of Baseball Leagues (NABL) claimed that she did not meet the physical requirements of the job. Gera filed a sex-discrimination case under Title VII of the Civil Rights Act with the New York State Human Rights Commission. She accused both the New York Professional Baseball League and its president, Vincent McNamara, of not employing her as an umpire due to her sex. Gera fought the NABL in court for five years. On January 13, 1972, Gera finally won a discrimination suit against the NABL. She received a contract to work in the New York–Penn League, opening the door for her to become the first female umpire in professional baseball. In 1972, she gained national attention when she umpired the first game of a Class A minor-league doubleheader between the Geneva Senators and the Auburn Twins.[1]

Major-league baseball still has not promoted a woman to umpire in the major leagues.

1972: Title IX, signed by then-president Richard Nixon, stated that no one can be discriminated against on the basis of gender within schools or other organizations that receive federal money. This move helped ensure that high schools and colleges cannot exclude females from participating in varsity sports.

Despite improvements stemming from Title IX there was still inequality in sports, especially in Little League Baseball. A New Jersey girl, Maria Pepe, sued Little League Baseball in order to play. The Supreme Court eventually ruled that Little League must give girls the opportunity to try out. This ruling put force behind Title IX.

1992: Camden Yards, the creation of Baltimore Orioles executive Janet Marie Smith, opened in Baltimore. Smith directed the design of the ballpark, which is now regarded as the pioneer of a new era of major-league parks. Camden Yards was only her first.

1992:   The movie *A League of Their Own* premiered and changed the lives of girls and women around the country as they watched women playing baseball on the big screen. The movie remains the largest-grossing baseball movie of all time.

1994:   Ila Borders became the first woman to pitch in a men's college baseball game. Three years later, she signed a professional contract with the St. Paul Saints of the independent Northern League.

1994:   Two years after the movie *A League of Their Own* became a sensation, professional women's baseball returned when the Colorado Silver Bullets team was formed by Bob Hope, a former Atlanta Braves executive. In the 1980s, he and his partners tried to field a women's minor-league team called the Sun Sox. He organized and held tryouts for the team, but the minor-league system would not allow the team into any league. In 1994, Hope secured $2 million dollars in sponsorship from Coors Brewing Company and, along with Hall of Famer Phil Niekro, who agreed to manage the team, the Silver Bullets held tryouts across the country.[2]

2006:   Effa Manley became the first woman inducted into the Baseball Hall of Fame.

2014:   Mo'ne Davis of Philadelphia became the first girl to win a game and pitch a shutout in the history of the Little League World Series, drawing national attention for girls in amateur baseball.

2014:   The IWBC was formed at the home of Maybelle Blair.

2017:   Claire Smith was named the winner of the prestigious BBWAA Career Excellence Award. She was the first woman to receive the honor.

2020:   The San Francisco Giants hired Alyssa Nakken as an on-field coach, making her the first female to hold such a position in the history of the major leagues.

2020:   The Miami Marlins hired Kim Ng as their new general manager. A longtime executive, Ng became the first woman to serve as a general manager in the major leagues.

2021:   Rachel Balkovec was hired as manager of the New York Yankees' affiliate in Tampa, Florida. Balkovec became the first full-time female manager of a minor-league team affiliated with Major League Baseball.

2021:   The Boston Red Sox hired Bianca Smith as a minor-league coach, making her the first Black woman to serve as a coach in the history of professional baseball.

2022:   Joining the Staten Island Ferry Hawks of the Atlantic League, Kelsie Whitmore became the first female player to sign a contract with a league affiliated with Major League Baseball.

2023:	Olivia Pichardo became the first woman to appear in an NCAA Division I baseball game when she pinch-hit for Brown University.
2024:	The Oakland As announced that Jenny Cavnar will become the first woman in major-league history to serve as a team's regular play-by-play broadcaster.
2024:	Kelsie Whitmore made history again when she became the first woman hired to play in the Pioneer League. She was chosen by the Oakland Ballers after an open tryout.

AUTHOR'S NOTE

I was present for many of Maybelle's later adventures. At the time that she and Shirley resigned from the AAGPBLPA board, I was president and also resigned. When they gathered in California to form the IWBC, I was there and became the organization's first president. I am currently the full-time CEO. During the writing of this book, I have tried to retell the stories about the AAGPBL and explain the growth of the IWBC in an unbiased manner. But I also want readers to know my own role in those events.

In 2020, when Will Graham and Abbi Jacobson reached out to Maybelle about consulting on their new show about the women of the AAGPBL, they also sought historic information that I could provide. I played a very minor role in advising them, but I do want to be honest about my own part in that process and my participation in all the events discussed in Maybelle's biography.

NOTES

INTRODUCTION

1. Blair interviews, April 21–24, 2021. All Blair quotes that follow are from this interview, unless otherwise cited.

2. Remy Tumin, "Maybelle Blair Inspired 'A League of Their Own.' At 95, She's Far from Done," *New York Times*, published July 4, 2022, updated July 7, 2022, https://www.nytimes.com/2022/07/04/sports/baseball/maybelle-blair-a-league-of-their-own.html.

3. Emma Hrubi, "'A League of Their Own': Meet 95-Year-Old Who Helped Inspire Amazon Series," justwomenssports.com, January 9, 2023, https://justwomenssports.com/league-of-their-own-maybelle-blair-amazon-prime-s/.

4. Emma Baccellieri, "From 'A League of Their Own' to Building a Museum of Their Own," *Sports Illustrated*, March 5, 2021, https://www.si.com/mlb/2021/01/11/international-womens-baseball-center-illinois.

5. Stacy Lamb, "'A League of Their Own' Inspiration Maybelle Blair on Coming Out at 95 & New Amazon Series," *Entertainment Tonight*, June 16, 2023, https://www.etonline.com/a-league-of-their-own-inspiration-maybelle-blair-on-coming-out-at-95-new-amazon-series-exclusive.

6. Amelia Earhart quote about achievement, March 4, 2024, https://quotequeendom.com/amelia-earhart-quotes.

CHAPTER 1

1. Blair interviews, April 21–24, 2021. All Blair quotes that follow are from this interview, unless otherwise cited.

2. The Defenders, "Heroes Who Died Fighting for Freedom," "Remember, Battle and Revolution," October 2, 2022, tps://www.thealamo.org/remember/battle-and-revolution/defenders.

3. The Defenders, "Heroes Who Died Fighting for Freedom," "Remember, Battle and Revolution," October 2, 2022, tps://www.thealamo.org/remember/battle-and-revolution/defenders.

4. Clay Coppedge, *Texas Baseball: A Lone Star Diamond History from Town Teams to the Big Leagues* (History Press, 2012), 10.

5. Coppedge, 10.

6. Gai Berlage, *Women in Baseball: The Forgotten History* (Praeger, 1994), 134.

7. Blair used "infantile paralysis" to describe Bud's childhood disease. It is more commonly known as polio now.

CHAPTER 2

1. Jose M. Alamillo, *Deportes: The Making of a Sporting Mexican Diaspora (Latinidad: Transnational Cultures in the United States)* (Rutgers University Press, 2020), 167.

2. Maureen O'Donnell, "National Girls Baseball League's 'Kotch' Kowell Dead at 91," *Chicago Sun-Times*, accessed March 7, 2024.

3. Jerry Crimmins, "Girls Baseball League Founder Emery A. Parichy," *Chicago Tribune*, March 19, 2024.

4. Judith Adkins, "These People Are Frightened to Death," National Archives, March 12, 2023, https://www.archives.gov/publications/prologue/2016/summer/lavender.html.

5. Judith Adkins, "These People Are Frightened to Death," March 12, 2023.

CHAPTER 3

1. Blair interviews, April 21–24, 2021. All Blair quotes that follow are from this interview, unless otherwise cited.

2. Jeneane Lesko, "League History," Official Website of the AAGPBL: All American Girls Professional Baseball League Players Association, November 9, 2015, www.aagpbl.org/index.cfm/pages/league/12/league-history.

3. Jeneane Lesko, "League History," Official Website of the AAGPBL: All American Girls Professional Baseball League Players Association, November 9, 2015, www.aagpbl.org/index.cfm/pages/league/12/league-history.

4. This is a list of the teams and the years they were in existence: Kenosha Comets (1943–1951), Racine Belles (1943–1950), Rockford Peaches (1943–1954), South Bend Blue Sox (1943–1954), Milwaukee Chicks (1944), Minneapolis Millerettes (1944), Fort Wayne Daisies (1945–1954), Grand Rapids Chicks (1945–1954), Muskegon Lassies (1946–1949), Peoria Redwings (1946–1951), Chicago Colleens (1948), Springfield Sallies (1948), Kalamazoo Lassies (1950–1954), Battle Creek Belles (1951–1952), Muskegon Belles (1953).

CHAPTER 4

1. Seal Paterson, "Beer Me," My New Orleans, February 10, 2024, https://www.myneworleans.com/beer-me/.
2. Ralph Vartabedian, "Former Northrop CEO Thomas V. Jones Dies at 93," *Los Angeles Times*, February 11, 2024, https://www.latimes.com/local/obituaries/la-xpm-2014-jan-08-la-me-thomas-jones-20140109-story.html.
3. Lillian Faderman, *Gay L.A.: A History of Sexual Outlaws, Power Politics, and Lipstick Lesbians* (University of California Press, 2006), 90.
4. Faderman, 91.
5. Faderman, 91.
6. Rod Blair, interview by Kat D. Williams, April 30, 2024.
7. Rod Blair, interview, April 30, 2024.
8. Rod Blair, interview, April 30, 2024.
9. Rod Blair, interview, April 30, 2024.
10. Rod Blair, interview, April 30, 2024.
11. Rod Blair, interview, April 30, 2024.
12. Rod Blair, interview, April 30, 2024.
13. Rod Blair, interview, April 30, 2024.

CHAPTER 5

1. Blair interviews, April 21–24, 2021. All Blair quotes that follow are from this interview, unless otherwise cited.
2. Ed Des Lauriers, as quoted in Merrie A. Fidler, *Origins and History of the All-American Girls Professional Baseball League* (McFarland & Company, 2010), 229.
3. Fidler, *Origins and History*, 229–30.
4. Fidler, *Origins and History*, 231–32.
5. June Peppas, as quoted in Fidler, *Origins and History*, 232.
6. Ruth Davis, as quoted in Fidler, *Origins and History*, 236.
7. AAGPBL advertisement, as quoted in Fidler, *Origins and History*, 237.
8. Kelly Candaele, as quoted in Fidler, *Origins and History*, 279.
9. Fidler, *Origins and History*, 269–71.
10. From the AAGPBL Newsletter *Extra Innings* (April 1986), author's personal collection.
11. Fidler, *Origins and History*, 251.
12. Fidler, *Origins and History*, 258–59.
13. Ted Spencer, as quoted in Fidler, *Origins and History*, 259.

CHAPTER 6

1. Penny Marshall, foreword, in Jane Gottesman, *Game Face: What Does a Female Athlete Look Like?* (Random House, 2001), 9.

2. Penny Marshall, foreword, in Jane Gottesman, *Game Face: What Does a Female Athlete Look Like?* (Random House, 2001), 9.

3. Sam Bauman, "A League of Her Own: Part 2," uppermichiganssource.com, February 29, 2024, https://www.uppermichiganssource.com/content/news/A -League-of-Her-Own-Part-2-401258645.html.

4. Sam Bauman, "A League of Her Own: Part 2," uppermichiganssource.com, February 29, 2024, https://www.uppermichiganssource.com/content/news/A -League-of-Her-Own-Part-2-401258645.html.

5. Maybelle Blair, "Maybelle Blair," interview by James Smither, Veterans History Project, Digital Collections, Special Collections and University Archives, Grand Valley State University Libraries, 2009.

6. Terry Donahue, "Terry Donahue," interview by James Smither, Veterans History Project, Digital Collections, Special Collections and University Archives, Grand Valley State University Libraries, 2009.

7. *A League of Their Own*, directed by Penny Marshall, Parkway Productions, July 1992.

8. Shirley Burkovich, interview by the author, Palm Springs, CA, May 2021.

9. Shirley Burkovich, interview by the author, Palm Springs, CA, October 13, 2009.

10. https://baseballforall.com/, March 7, 2024.

11. Shirley Burkovich, informal conversation with the author, Orlando, FL, June 3, 2015.

CHAPTER 7

1. Donna Cohen, interview by the author, March 6, 2024.

2. "Diamond Find Veterans," *New York Times*, April 12, 1896, 3.

3. "Diamond Find Veterans," *New York Times*, April 12, 1896, 3.

4. Raymond Starr, "Book Review: A. G. Spalding and the Rise of Baseball," *Journal of San Diego History* (winter 1986), 32.

5. Blair interviews, April 21–24, 2021. All Blair quotes that follow are from this interview, unless otherwise cited.

CHAPTER 8

1. Feminist Majority Foundation's Task Force on Women and Girls in Sports, "Empowering Women in Sports," 1995, May 10, 2021, https://feminist.org /our-work/education-equity/gender-equity-in-athletics/empowering-women-in -sports/.

CHAPTER 9

1. Neptune's is a restaurant near where Blair lives in Sunset Beach, California.

2. Information about mid-twentieth-century lesbian dress and culture was attained from Elizabeth Lapovsky Kennedy and Madeline D. Davis, *Boots of Leather, Slippers of Gold: The History of a Lesbian Community* (Routledge, 1993).

3. 2019 Tribeca Film Festival highlights & ICYMI moments, Tribeca, May 29, 2024, archived from the original on September 19, 2020.

4. Rod Blair, interview by the author, April 2024.

5. Kevin Fallon, "The 22 Best TV Shows of 2022," April 6, 2024, https:// www.thedailybeast.com/obsessed/22-best-tv-shows-of-2022-from-better-call-saul -to-bravo?ref=wrap.

6. Linda Holmes, "A League of Their Own 2022 Amazon Prime," National Public Radio, April 6, 2024, https://www.npr.org/2022/08/11/1116855780/a -league-of-their-own-2022-amazon-prime-review.

7. Lia Beck, "A League of Their Own Reviews," Best Life Online, May 3, 2024, https://bestlifeonline.com/a-league-of-their-own-reviews-news/.

APPENDIX

1. National Baseball Hall of Fame, accessed May 30, 2024, https://baseballhall .org/women-in-baseball.

2. National Baseball Hall of Fame, accessed May 30, 2024, https://baseballhall .org/women-in-baseball.

AUTHOR-CONDUCTED
ORAL HISTORIES

Alvarez, Isabel "Lefty." Grand Rapids, MI, June 8, 2007.
———. Palm Springs, CA, June 11, 2011.
———. Via telephone, October 20, 2011.
Blair, Maybelle. Palm Springs, CA, January 24, 2008.
———. Palm Springs, CA, July 23, 2011.
———. Orlando, FL, June 2 and 3, 2015.
———. Sunset Beach, CA, April 21–24, 2021.
Burkovich, Shirley. Palm Springs, CA, January 23, 2008.
———. October 13, 2009.
———. Orlando, FL, June 2–3, 2015.
———. Palm Springs, CA, May 2021.
Donahue, Terry. Via telephone, June 10, 2007.
———. Via telephone, September 14, 2008.
Kunkel, Karen. Syracuse, NY, September 12, 2003.
Moffet, Jane. Cape May, NJ, May 9, 2006.
———. Detroit, MI, September 2010.

BIBLIOGRAPHY

All American Girls Professional Baseball League Collection. Baseball Hall of Fame
    Research Library, Cooperstown, NY.
Ardell, Jean. *Breaking into Baseball: Women and the National Past Time*. Southern
    Illinois Press, 2005.
Berlage, Gai. *Women in Baseball: The Forgotten History*. Praeger Publishers, 1994.
Browne, Lois. *The Girls of Summer: The Real Story of the All-American Girls
    Professional Baseball League*. HarperCollins, 1992.

Bullock, Steven R. *Playing for Their Nation: Baseball and the American Military during World War II*. University of Nebraska Press, 2004.

Colorado Silver Bullets. Colorado Springs, CO. http://www.coloradosilverbullets .org/.

Empowering Women in Sports. The Empowering Women Series, No. 4. Feminist Majority Foundation, 1995. Accessed December 15, 2015. feminist.org/researc h/sports/sports2.html.

Fidler, Merrie A. *The Origins and History of the All-American Girls Professional Baseball League*. McFarland, 2006.

Fidler, Merrie A. "The Development and Decline of the All-American Girls Baseball League, 1943–1954." Master of science thesis, University of Massachusetts, Amherst, 1976.

Fincher, Jack. "The 'Belles of the Game' Were a Hit with Their Fans." *Smithsonian* 20 (1999): 88–97.

Gregorich, Barbara. *Women at Play: The Story of Women in Baseball*. Harcourt, Brace and Company, 1993.

History Page. USA Baseball, Durham, NC. http://web.usabaseball.com/playball/ womens-baseball/history/.

Johnson, Susan E. *When Women Played Hardball*. Seal Press, 1994.

Litoff, Judy, and David Smith. *American Women in a World at War: Contemporary Accounts from World War II*. The Worlds of Women Series. Rowman & Littlefield, 1996.

Madden, W. C. *The All-American Girls Professional Baseball League Record Book: Comprehensive Hitting, Fielding and Pitching Statistics*. McFarland, 2000.

Madden, W. C. *The Women of the All-American Girls Professional Baseball League: A Biographical Dictionary*. McFarland, 1997.

Miller, Ernestine. *Making Her Mark: Firsts and Milestones in Women's Sports*. McGraw Hill Companies, 2002.

Muench, Matthew. "More Girls Playing High School Baseball." ESPN High School. http://espn.go.com/blog/high-school/baseball/post/_/id/519/chang ing-the-game-girls-in-high-school-baseball.

Official Website of the AAGPBL: All-American Girls Professional Baseball League Players Association. aagpbl.org/index.cfm.

Osborne, Carol A., and Fiona Skillen. *Women in Sports History*. Routledge, 2012.

Park, Roberta J., and Patricia Vertinsky. *Women, Sport, Society: Further Reflections, Reaffirming Mary Wollstonecraft*. Routledge, 2011.

Pierman, Carol J. "Baseball, Conduct, and True Womanhood." *Women's Studies Quarterly* 33, no. ½ (spring 2005): 60–85.

Pierman, Carol J. "The All-American Girls Professional Baseball League: Accomplishing Great Things in a Dangerous World." In *Across the Diamond: Essays on Baseball and American Culture*, edited by Edward J. Rielly, 97–108. Haworth, 2003.

Roepke, Sharon. *Diamond Gals*. Self-published, 1986.

Tucker Institute for Research on Girls and Women in Sport, University of Minnesota. July 20, 2019. cehd.umn.edu/tuckercenter/research/default.html.

Veterans History Project. Special Collections and University Archives, Grand Valley State University Libraries, Allendale, MI.cdm16015.contentdm.oclc.org/cdm/singleitem/collection/p15068coll11/id/8/rec/3.

Women's Sports Foundation website. www.womenssportsfoundation.org/.

INDEX

ABOUT THE AUTHOR

Dr. Kat Williams is a professor emeritus at Marshall University, where she has taught women's and sport history for twenty-three years. She was a founder and the first president of the IWBC. She now serves as the organization's CEO. Kat is the author of several articles about women's sport, including "Sport: 'A Useful Category of Historical Analysis,'" and two books, *The All-American Girls after the AAGPBL* and *Isabel Lefty Alvarez: The Improbable Life of a Cuban American Baseball Star*. Through teaching, scholarship, and advocacy, Kat is dedicated to the preservation of women's sport history and to helping girls become independent, confident leaders.

www.ingramcontent.com/pod-product-compliance
Lightning Source LLC
Chambersburg PA
CBHW070920150426
42812CB00048B/1137